THE CRAFTSMAN'S ART SERIES

The Craft of Embroidery

GW00746006

The Craftsman's Art Series

The Craft of
Embroidery

Pat Phillpott

Pat Phillpott

August 1977.

Stanley Paul, London

Stanley Paul & Co Ltd
3 Fitzroy Square, London W1

An imprint of the Hutchinson Publishing Group

London Melbourne Sydney Auckland
Wellington Johannesburg and agencies
throughout the world

First published 1976
© Pat Phillpott 1976
Drawings © Stanley Paul & Co Ltd

Printed in Great Britain by The Anchor Press Ltd
and bound by Wm Brendon & Son Ltd
both of Tiptree, Essex

ISBN 09 127570 9
     09 127571 7

Photographs throughout by Reg Marles

Contents

Preface

This book is an introduction to the basic skills of embroidery. My aim has been to give you a confident start to one of the most exciting modern crafts. I have tried to keep to the practical approach which should give you a firm structure on which to build later. The individual chapters deal with topics and methods separately. Once you have finished your first piece, you will need to use each chapter rather like a separate reference book, until the skills become automatic.

Inspiration for writing the book arose from some eight years of teaching mature students in colleges of further education. I should like to thank my students, past and present, particularly at the Mid-Warwickshire College of Further Education for testing and using my ideas and contributing many of their own.

Detail of 'The Lake District' embroidery by the author

This group of embroideries
all use simple stitches. They
are inspired by a photograph
(1) (2); by the fabric itself
(3) (4); or are developed
from a drawing, which
results in a different quality
in the embroidery (5) (6).

1

2

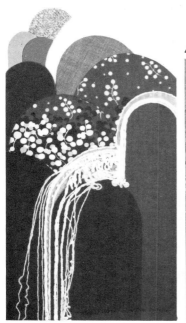

4

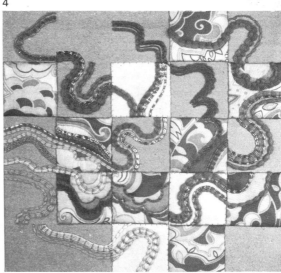

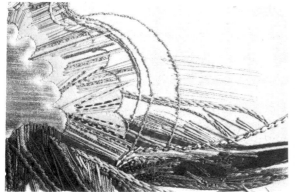

5

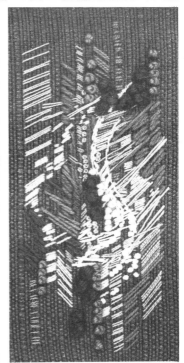

6

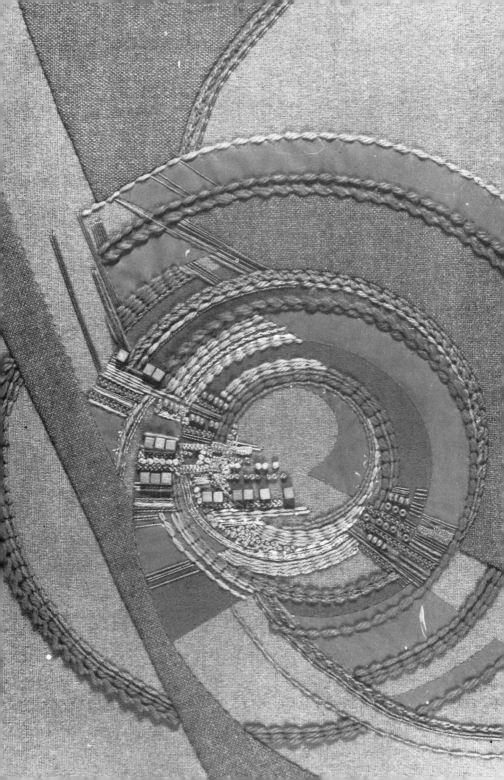

1. Embroidery - an introduction

The word 'embroidery' has been used for so long it is difficult to find a better one which has the right meaning. A dictionary is likely to say 'ornament with needlework' or 'embellishment, exaggeration': this interpretation is not quite true any longer. We do still decorate or embellish as one might on a dress or tray cloth but we go further today and say that a piece of embroidery may be designed in its own right and conceived as a whole. Such items may be designed to hang on the wall (these are usually called 'panels'), or as three-dimensional objects to be viewed from all angles (usually called 'soft sculpture' or 'structures'), and the finished product should be considered an art form just as valid as painting and sculpture.

Traditional embroidery was rather flat, and threads of different types were not mixed in the same piece of work. The embroidery was designed as decoration and was influenced by design and traditions of the time. Often the colours were naturalistic and the use of stitches unimaginative. Embroiderers thought more of the therapeutic satisfaction in the work and not the design. Embroidery was used mostly to decorate practical articles like chair seats, curtains, aprons, dresses, waistcoats, shoes, tray cloths, towels, books and boxes. The transfer patterns of today have been inherited from those times; a border of flowers was transferred on to whatever you wanted to embroider and the same one could be used for quite different articles.

There is far more satisfaction to be gained from designing and developing your own ideas and doing them specifically for a particular piece: this is what I mean by 'conceived as a whole'. Transfers are not so satisfying for three different articles, each of which may require a slight variation in the designs with different proportions and different stitches.

'Roundabout' panel by the author in reds and pinks on gold, using screen printing on the background fabric, pvc, hand stitching and wooden beads

Previously some embroidery has imitated other textiles that were imported into this country and were expensive. Hence the word 'tapestry' instead of 'canvas work' (the correct term) because the large wall hangings imitated the tapestry weaving, and we find embroidery imitating printed material for bed hangings. You must not try to copy other media – embroidery must be embroidery.

If you are frightened of 'plunging in at the deep end' why not try out some new stitches that you did not previously know, and new or different threads on a transfer: preferably something simple that you could even add to – certainly you could mix wools and silks.

The modern approach could almost be said to be painting with fabric and threads. This can be abstract or realistic, but whatever it is you can see immediately that there are different stitches and different fabric textures. The design can be big, bold and simple or it can be 'representational'. In all cases you will find that surface effects are emphasized. Several fabrics and several types of embroidery can be used together, some creating three dimensions. Areas of fabric are used very boldly as though you had painted areas of colour before working into the sections you wish to emphasize; no longer need you work with the same detail all over. This is why you must plan your embroidery so that shape, tone, colour, line and texture are all in the right places.

Whatever the embroidery it must preserve the essential qualities of threads and fabric. These are their relief: they stand out from the background and their textural qualities vary. You must want to touch the finished product. Because the thread sits on top of the fabric it will cast a shadow from its thickness. This creates the relief effect. Beads, french knots and padding fabric will achieve the same result.

In modern embroidery disciplined experiment is the key to success. Before you reach this stage you must practise the different techniques involved. This book does not offer an exhaustive treatment of all the possibilities, but it gives an introduction to some of the most important you will need to learn before branching out on your own. There are two important things you must always remember. First, you will have to develop a 'seeing eye' to expand your visual sense. Start looking at things. Have you noticed the way reflections on windows and shiny surfaces are distorted into wavy patterns? Have you noticed the shapes of stones in an old wall, or the grouping of cows in a field?

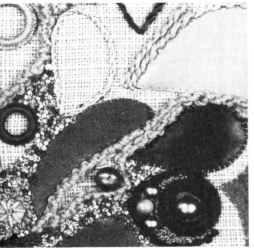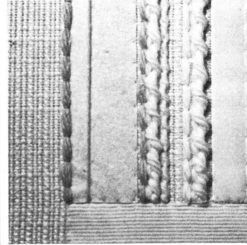

From an embroidery by Carol Hill   From an embroidery by the author

Secondly, you must think of embroidery as a language. It is impossible to translate from one language into another absolutely; you can get the same feeling, the atmosphere or the quality of something, but you cannot reproduce it exactly. In the same way the embroiderer takes qualities and moods and translates them into stitches and fabrics.

You cannot make an embroidered flower look exactly like a real flower. It is the same with birds, trees or landscapes. In embroidery you should be looking out for textures, surfaces, tonal values or relief, and use those, emphasizing the qualities you like. This is where your personality enters into it. Take a flower, for example. It can have all sorts of qualities which intrigue you. Is it the colour, the shape of the petals, the way the petals curl up giving a three-dimensional quality to the form, the transparent frailness of the petals or the line patterns on them? This is an important question because your piece of work will preserve those qualities that catch your eye. Another person may notice and like something else about that flower. The composition could still be realistic while remaining essentially a design for embroidery. Perhaps those who like abstract designs will benefit because they are not trying to copy but to take the essence of a subject.

'Reflections' panel by Dorothy Barrowman

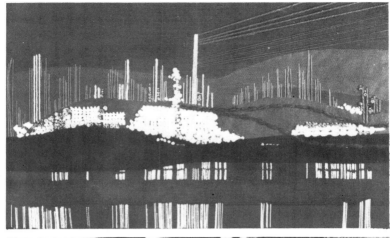

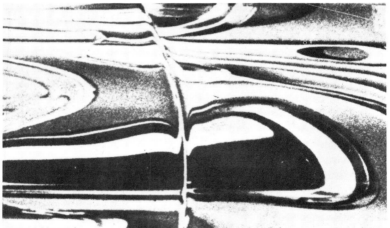

Reflections and flower, two contrasting sources of inspiration

Detail from an embroidery of Geraniums by Flo Tallis

Embroidery is based on several traditional techniques most of which have now changed and developed: for instance, blackwork, canvas work, gold work, drawn thread, and pulled work. We are lucky to have so much to draw on. In painting it would be very difficult to mix the bulk and strength of oil paint with the transparent quality of water colour. In embroidery you can do this mixing quite· successfully; tweeds and velvets can be put together with nets and other transparent fabrics in the same piece of work. It is possible to combine techniques as diverse as quilting and canvas work, gold work and pulled work, and if they require different fabrics as a background you can join two or three together before beginning the stitchery.

All the techniques have very different qualities which you can use in your interpretation. The techniques already mentioned are more advanced. In this book I start at the beginning. The techniques looked at are the basic ones – appliqué, stitchery and padding – since these are the foundations of embroidery. Freedom of expression will come with experience. Techniques need to be learnt along with methods of designing in order to give you the confidence to make your own designs. After all, the design needs to be simple and well balanced if the techniques and textures are to be interesting.

Equipment

One or two basic pieces are necessary but other items can be acquired

'Bonfire' panel worked by Pat Hardy in black, red and white. This ranges from work that is quite heavy to the net areas and fine fluffy threads indicating the smoke

'Circles' panel designed and worked by Mrs Rickards. This uses appliqué, needleweaving and some knots. It is in dark plums, pinks and mauves

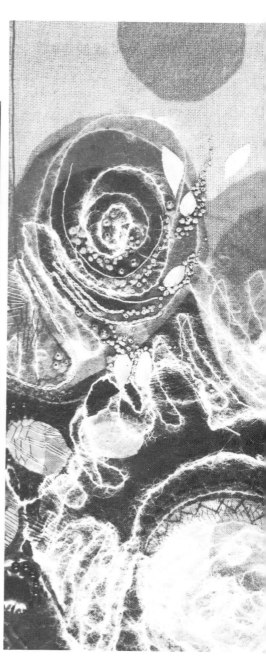

'Ink Blot' panel worked by Pat Hardy from an ink blot on paper. Here canvaswork, needleweaving, pulled work and free stitchery have been used as well as the background fabric being cut into holes with a colour behind.

later. None of them should be expensive except perhaps good-quality scissors.

A frame

A frame is really necessary to keep the fabric taut while working. Not everybody uses one, but once you have and discovered the advantages you will probably find you cannot work without one. You can use both hands while sewing, making the work quicker and more accurate. The frame is either supported between two surfaces (tables, or table and chair) or clamped to the edge of the table. One hand can be used underneath the work, the other above, or both hands can be free above, to manipulate difficult threads. You can view the whole piece of work from the beginning, not just the small areas you are working on, and this, if you are taking embroidery seriously, is absolutely necessary. If you work with a limp piece of fabric in your hands the stitches will be less accurate, the tension uneven and, most important, lines that should be straight will probably waver. In the end you will be more professional with a frame. There are basically three types to choose from;

A hoop. This is a small round embroidery frame tensioned by a screw. For small experiments, or for projects like bags or cushion covers where the work will not stay stretched on a frame when it is finished, 8, 9 or 10 in./20, 23, 25 cm are the most useful.

Hoops for use at the machine or small pieces of hand embroidery. One shows its centre ring bound in fabric to make a firmer grip and damage the fabric less

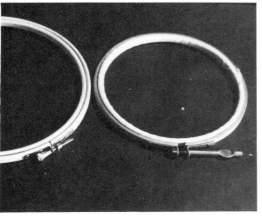

A slate frame.   This is not very satisfactory because you have to remount the embroidery after working. It is likely that the tension on the frame cannot be repeated exactly when mounting and so the embroidery loses its crispness. It is useful, though, for canvas work where you do not want to stitch over the wood.

Slate frame

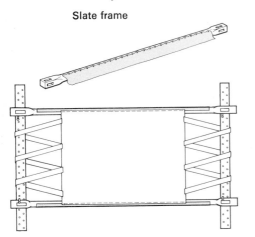

Homemade frame

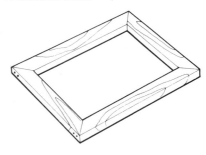

One hand underneath making work easier

A rectangular 'home-made' frame   is like a simple picture frame: the outside dimensions are the size of the embroidery and the finished work stays on the frame. This is basically the best type of frame for panels destined to be hung on a wall and admired as pictures. The embroidery is not moved once it has been stapled or tacked on, therefore the work never changes its form and tension, and long stitches can be used with confidence.

Scissors

You will need a good pair of large cutting-out dressmaking shears, a small, fine, pointed pair and a curved small pair for unpicking, trimming and general work. Ideally none of these should be used for anything else (except dressmaking). You should keep an old pair for cutting paper.

Needles

Various sizes of crewel (sharp-pointed with long eyes) and tapestry needles (flatter and less sharp). You will need several really large ones. Remember the needle has to make a hole large enough to take *two* strands of thread, not one, through the fabric. Therefore, take a needle you think looks too big and it will probably be just right. If the hole is not large enough you wear the thread and tug at the fabric getting it through, the result is an uneven tension. With the right needle, though the hole may seem large, the fabric closes in again. 'Knitter's needles' sold for sewing up knitting are good for thick threads.

Materials

Once you have become serious about this subject it is as well to be systematic about collecting things like fabric pieces, beads and threads.

Keep reels of machine thread separately.

Clear polythene bags are good for fabrics and for larger balls of wool. Clear glass jars will store beads, and shoe boxes will take skeins of threads, all segregated by colour. Fabrics big enough for background pieces (squares of 12–15 in./30–40 cm upwards) should be stored separately. Firm fabrics are suitable for backgrounds. Remember they have to stay stretched on the frame and support the work as you do it. The most useful are furnishing fabrics, twill-weave cottons, denims, dress and skirt-weight wools, terylene and worsteds. Avoid all knitted fabrics for backgrounds as they stretch.

All fabrics can be used in appliqué on top. And for this you should collect really interesting weaves and textures: tweeds, corduroys, satins. The more you have in each colour range the more interesting your work will be. Contrast is essential. Add to your collection all the time, as bargains and sales crop up. A bag or box for miscellaneous things that you can use in your work is a good idea. Washers, straws, curtain rings, insides of packaging may all be used one day.

You will also at some time require simple, neutral backing fabrics which you might as well buy when you see them cheap on a sale counter – curtain lining, calico, cotton, lawn – anything that will serve as a support to another fabric which is too thin itself, or as a backing to padding. Kapok is useful for quilting on panels or pictures; synthetic wadding is good for quilting on washable articles or 'all-over' quilting when using sheets of wadding. Iron-on interfacing is good for preventing fabrics fraying (e.g. in appliqué), for holding threads on the wrong side of the work, and for stiffening.

Threads

Anything can be used provided it will not rot or deteriorate: string, ribbons, raffia, cords as well as actual threads. Remember you are aiming at producing something that will last. If anything is too thick to go into the needle you must work out how to use it on the surface, stitching it down with a thinner thread. These are the main threads available:

Machine thread. For zigzag machining and very fine hand work.

Buttonhole twist on a reel. For bolder machine work and thin lines of hand embroidery.

Lurex threads (*on reels for machining*). Flat threads in general go on to the spool (which may need loosening slightly), round ones can often go through the largest needle (remember to loosen the top tension).

Soft embroidery cotton. This has a dull finish but rubs up and goes fluffy.

Coton Perlé No. 5. Generally available. English in balls, French in skeins. It has a shiny twist and is good for practical pieces. It does not go dull with use. You can also use it in a machine spool.

Coton Perlé No. 8. Fine, a little thicker than buttonhole twist.

Coton Perlé No. 3. Thick, only available by DMC (a French company whose products are sold here). It is very good thread, lovely to use; so far there is nothing like it in English threads.

Cotton à broder. A softer, nor so twisted cotton thread as thick as perlé No. 8.

Stranded cotton. Always easy to get; good for use in a single strand or a small number of strands but not good using the full six at once. You will find the tension of the strands is uneven as you work.

Raffia/raffine. Shiny and dull versions available from arts and crafts shops, lampshade-making departments, etc. Very strong and easily used with a large needle (knitter's needle) either as it is or flattening for each stitch which gives it a more transparent look (and makes it more fragile).

Crewel wool. In skeins or hanks by bulk. This is a fine twisted wool and you can use it as a stranded thread as thick as you need. Good colours.

Tapestry wool. These can either be full thickness, as made by D M C, Penelope, and Appletons, or stranded as supplied by the Royal School of Needlework for you to vary the thickness. They have a dull plain twist.

Knitting wool. Plain four-ply, double-knitting: most of these are as good as tapestry wool and much cheaper, especially in skeins. The only time to consider carefully whether to use knitting wool is when doing canvas work for chair seats on which wear would be considerable. It is nearly always washable if it is for ordinary knitting in the first place. Crêpe has a more interesting texture and tighter twist. It therefore does not fluff up so much and shows stitches up better.

Nylon knitting wool. Interesting because nylon gives dull surface appearance, but stretches as you work; avoid it if you are a complete beginner.

Tricel crêpe. A shiny version of crêpe knitting yarn. Good when used with dull threads to show up the shine; very strong and washable. It tends to stretch and work a bit thinner, so you might need to use it double.

Chunky knitting wools. The cheapest thick threads and easily available. There are others for embroidery but they are expensive. Some are smooth and firm, some soft and twisted: the latter fluff out and produce a very thick stitch. The largest knitter's needle must be used.

Chunky knitting wools (man-made-fibre type). These look the same as wool but tend, like the tricel wool, to work thinner; use double if you want a really thick line. They are usually cheaper than wool.

Crochet threads. All are good for embroidery as they are usually firmly twisted, washable and show a stitch up beautifully. They can be dull cotton or shiny man-made fibre.

Crochet lurex threads. These are very useful but are often made like a chain and come undone as you work. If they do, thread a large needle and tie a knot at both ends. The needle will make a hole large enough to pull through the extra knot as you work.

Strings. Useful and interesting when used on top in various 'couching' methods, or for making cords.

Cords. The shiny cords are good because they are glossier than normal embroidery threads and therefore give contrast. The normal cord from haberdashery departments can be destranded (untwisted) dipped in water and dried to remove the twist. You then have a much thinner one as well.

Ribbons. All sorts are useful. If you intend to use them on articles likely to be washed or dry cleaned all ribbons except nylon must be washed first.

Braids. These can often be unravelled for interesting threads if they are too formal in themselves.

Materials for designing

You will need paper, pencils, felt tip pens, a ruler, rubber and/or erasing fluid (such as Tipp-Ex), and scissors for paper-cutting; later you will probably use coloured inks, paints or wax crayons.

Transparent greaseproof paper is required for tracing, and usually for transferring an enlarged design, using the tacking method; use a felt tip pen for the tracing you are going to tack through.

Sheets of dressmaking pattern paper are good for keeping a full-size finished design on when your work is large.

Graph paper is useful when working to scale on a design to be reduced or enlarged.

Photographs from glossy magazines can be cut up to make a design combined with plain white or coloured paper: for this some form of adhesive to fix the various pieces of design on to a base sheet is needed: various forms are available – such as Gloy, Copydex, Cow-gum.

Making a start

Start a scrap-book: this will be your main source of inspiration. Collect illustrations that you like. They will not be complete designs for embroidery; you can take part of a picture. Take and cut a square hole in a piece of blank paper, then use the resulting 'frame' to inspect the photographs or illustrations you have collected. You will find that details from photographs will make interesting sources of design for embroidery. The hole cut out of the blank paper can be a different shape. Alternatively, you could cut two 'L' corners from a sheet of paper and use them together as an adjustable 'frame'.

Your scrap-book can be divided into sections for shape, line, texture, colour, landscape, animals, or plants.

2. Looking at Stitches

Although there are a great number of stitches available you do not need to know them all. No longer does a stitch have to be even: it should change as you want it to, so that you can make a fat or thin line as you wish. You may develop a liking for a few favourite stitches. It is not the number of stitches you know which matters, but the way you use and vary a few. These can be infinitely elaborated by stretching them outwards or lengthways. You can also bend a stitch or turn it sideways to create movement. Combine a good use of threads with these variations and you will feel you have four times as much to choose from. If you are working on a frame you need not worry about the length of stitches on the right or the wrong side of the work, nor about the look of the wrong side. Starting with a knot at the other end of the thread is perfectly acceptable except perhaps on chair seats, or cushion covers that get a lot of hard wear.

Stitches fall into three categories, those making lines, 'linear stitches', those for textures 'broken stitches' (used separately), and 'all-over' stitches.

Linear stitches

Practically every stitch can be worked continuously forming a line.

The basic stitches

Flat stitches

1. Buttonhole (blanket)
2. Cretan stitch
3. Herringbone stitch
4. Ladder chain (open chain)
5. Feather stitch
6. Roumanian stitch
7. Vandyke stitch

Chain stitches

14. Cable chain
15. Chain stitch
16. Twisted-chain stitch (coral)

Knotted stitches

8. Double-knot stitch
9. Knotted-cable chain
10. Portuguese knotted-stem stitch

Smooth stitches

11. Couching
12. Running stitch (straight stitches)
13. Stem stitch

Thick stitches

17. Portuguese border stitch
18. Raised-chain band
19. Woven stem-stitch band
20. Rosette chain

The stitch and ideas on their variations

In order to understand anything you have to try it for yourself. So first you should learn each stitch, making a traditional sampler worked in rows of stitches 3 to 4 in./8 to 10 cm long. Try each stitch in this book in two very different thicknesses of thread such as chunky knitting wool and then perlé No. 5, or a crochet cotton. You will see immediately the difference in effect produced by variation in the thickness of thread. Once you have learnt the stitch you can consider ways of varying it. Think of stretching it, widening it and distorting it wherever possible.

If you wish to experiment further towards the freer approach, look at the inspirational photographs in your scrap-book. Decide on the quality a stitch has and then look for a picture having that quality. On examination you will begin to see that it is not the same texture all over, so you do not make the stitch the same from one end of a line to another.

Flat stitches

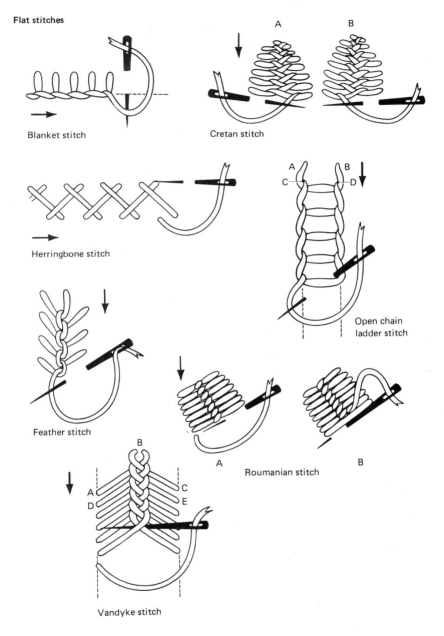

Blanket stitch

Cretan stitch

Herringbone stitch

Open chain
ladder stitch

Feather stitch

Roumanian stitch

Vandyke stitch

Knotted stitches

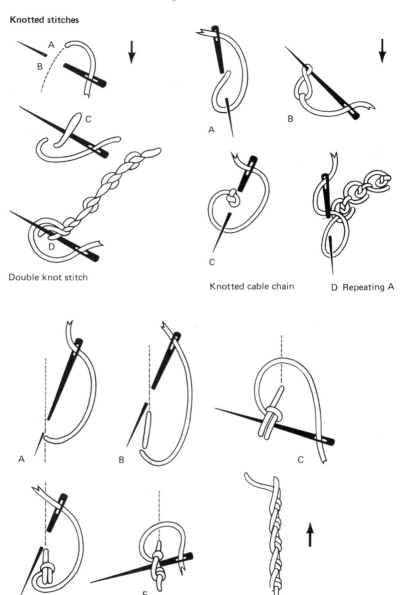

Double knot stitch

Knotted cable chain   D Repeating A

Portuguese knotted stem stitch

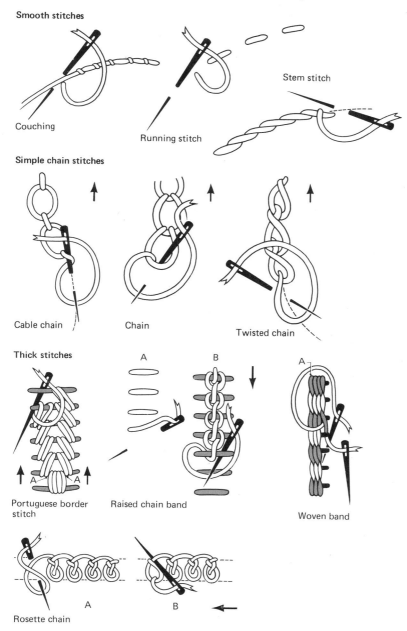

Smooth stitches

Couching

Running stitch

Stem stitch

Simple chain stitches

Cable chain

Chain

Twisted chain

Thick stitches

A B

A

Portuguese border stitch

Raised chain band

Woven band

A B

Rosette chain

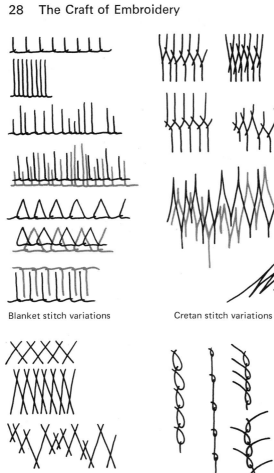

Blanket stitch variations

Cretan stitch variations

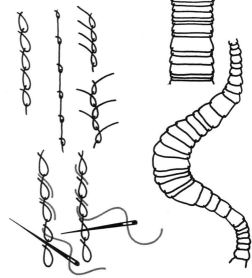

Herringbone stitch variations

Twisted chain variations

Ladder chain
creating movement

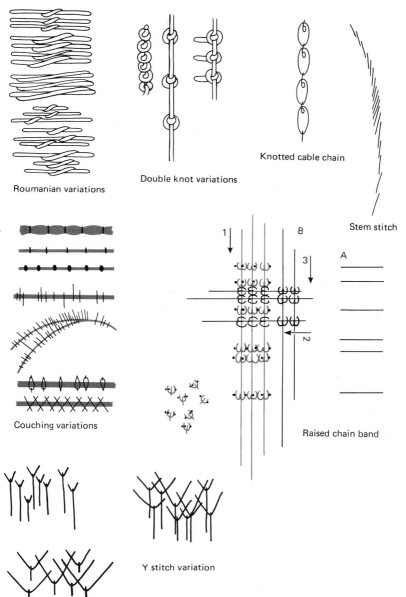

Roumanian variations

Double knot variations

Knotted cable chain

Stem stitch

Couching variations

Raised chain band

Y stitch variation

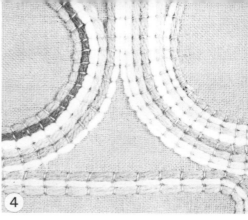

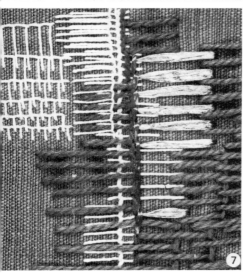

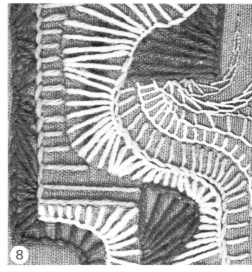

Details from experiments in one stitch:
1. French knots
2. Bullion knots
3. Raised chain band and
   Portuguese border stitch
4. Couching
5. Chain stitches
6. Cretan stitch
7. Blanket stitch
8. Blanket stitch
9. Herringbone stitch
10. Straight stitches
11. Straight stitches

Opposite page: Man-made line
patterns – a contrast to 'Natural
Lines'
Dead Hosta leaves and heather
root, a natural line pattern

Thicknesses and types of thread

Collect a range of threads of one colour and work a small embroidery from one section of the photo, looking through a cut-out square or circle in a piece of paper approximately 2 in./5 cm, no larger or the area of photograph gets too complicated. Work on a smooth fabric which will throw up the stitchery.

Tack a 6–8 in./15–20 cm square or circle in the centre of your fabric and work within that, starting with the main line and then working on either side of it. Make the contrasts more exaggerated with the thickness of the thread.

At some stage before you have finished put the photograph to one side and add more to what you have done so far, repeating a line that looks good, or putting a very thin one near a very thick one, or overlapping a thinner or shinier one over another. Leave some fabric between some lines to show them up.

The more you tackle the more you will realize the possibilities of stitches.

These little pieces can be mounted as panels (pictures) or greetings cards. You should finish with some interesting work.

Line: a closer look at design

A line can have many qualities – straight, wavy, curved, broken, dotted, knobbly, spiky, knotted and so on.

Look now at some pictures that seem to be made up of lines – the photographs above or any in your scrap-book. Observe the way lines are grouped and the effect of the spaces between them. Not all the

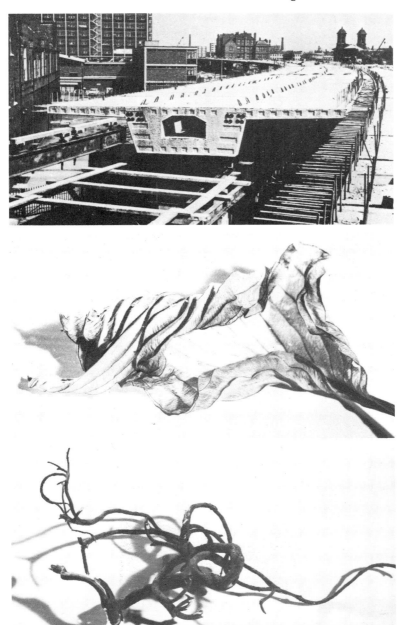

Pattern

Composition

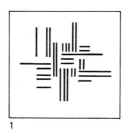

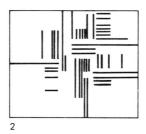

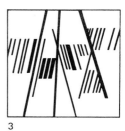

1

2

3

1. Floating space round the outside
2. Composition supported by long lines
3. Space to balance interest

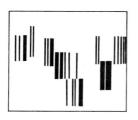

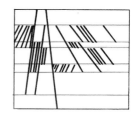

lines are the same, not all the spaces equal. If everything is even it is boring.

Interest is held by the variation in the lines and spaces. The grouping draws your attention to one place or another, thus beginning the idea of a focal point and a composition which can hold your attention.

You now have to look at the relationship, not just between the lines, but between the lines and the outside edge of your work. This is called a composition. When two lines are close together you 'read' them as one: there is a pull between them. Similarly there is a pull between them and the outside edge. If a line goes close to the edge it appears to pull outwards even more. This can mean that your eye is taken away from the focal area: care must be taken. A change of colour can bring your eye back.

If lines go off the edge, they stop the design from floating. Try to avoid floating space, whether you are considering a cushion cover, the bodice of a dress, or a panel to hang on the wall. They are all compositions with different outside shapes.

Space is very necessary but not floating round the outer edges. You need some plain areas left in order to show up the worked areas, otherwise your embroidery will be congested and not easy to look at. Think of it as balancing scales: whenever you work one area leave another plain. Remember, too, that the fabric is as important as the stitchery.

You might try out some of these ideas to help you make a 'linear' design. Your results could then be enlarged and used as the basis for an embroidery.

Take a 3 in./7·5 cm strip of paper and with a felt tip pen draw lines across it from one end to the other. The lines should be different widths and spaces, and all in one colour. Cut this strip up into pieces (parallel with the lines). Draw a 12 in./30 cm square on a sheet of paper with the same colour.

Keeping the lines vertical and parallel arrange the pieces so that you have some relationship between them as a composition in your square. Decide where your area of interest (focal point) is. When you have the final result stick the pieces to the paper.

You may need to cut some pieces smaller (with fewer lines on) and you could overlap if you want to, or make some lines thicker, or add a second colour where you think the focal area is.

Try repeating this exercise, adding some long lines either from the

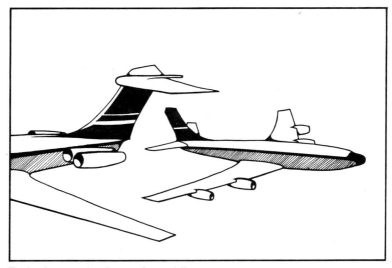

Tracing from an advertisement for an airline company.

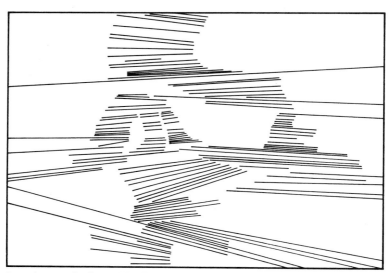

Retracing over the first making line patterns follow the shapes —
sometimes in the spaces — sometimes in the shapes.

Detail from panel by Ann Hatton, in greens and yellows, using only straight stitches

inside to the outside and/or from edge to edge, some thin, some thick. Watch where you put your thick ones. Not too near the outside. What is the difference between the two? Which do you prefer and why?

Now draw a rectangle or circle for your outer limit. Within this draw several horizontal lines at interesting intervals. Put a piece of tracing paper over this and doodle with lines at angles, stopping and starting on your horizontals, some going from top to bottom, some extending to the next horizontal and so on, varying as you wish. If this is on tracing paper you can keep trying until you achieve one you like. Decide on your focal area and emphasize it with closer or thicker lines, or lines going at a different angle.

Lay a piece of tracing paper over a simple photograph and draw a series of straight lines over this, relating to the spaces as well as the shapes.

If you try these ideas on paper it should not be difficult to enlarge your drawing (see p. 66) and then relate the thick lines to thick flat stitches or braids, ribbons and tapes, and the others to knotted stitches when you want to emphasize a line, or smooth thinner lines when you want them to be less important.

Broken stitches

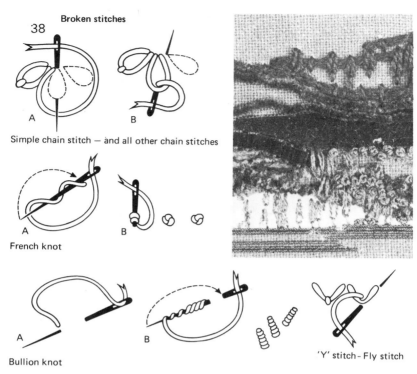

Simple chain stitch — and all other chain stitches

French knot

Bullion knot

'Y' stitch - Fly stitch

Texture stitches

Texture stitches are broken stitches, or stitches worked on top of each other at a different angle or with a different thread (e.g. raised-chain band or cretan stitch.)

You can now take a stitch and work it in varying sizes, combining contrasting threads, bringing the stitch close and opening it up, thus building an interesting area of relief. For instance you will find quite a difference between french knots worked in cord and next to it french knots in perlé No. 5. The difference in thread will make the stitch itself look different.

The basic stitches

Broken stitches	*All-over stitches used to overlap each other*
Chain stitches of all sorts	
French knots	Herringbone
Bullion knots	Cretan
Fly stitches	Raised-chain band
'Y' stitches Seeding	Buttonhole

Texture – a closer look

The texture of a work of art refers to the quality of its surface representation. This can be an all-over, ready-made surface, such as fabrics, wallpapers or wood have. It can also be a surface you create yourself, emphasizing the qualities you like.

Try to find photographs and sections of photographs which show definite textures. Look at them carefully. Is the texture shown in little lines, spots, blobs or a mixture of two? Are the marks fat at one end and thin at the other? Do the marks come in groups or form a linear pattern, or is everything completely random?

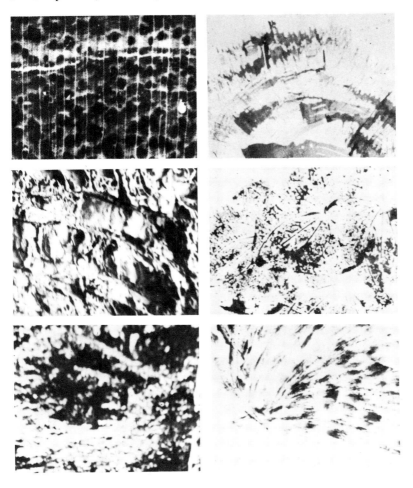

Try to decide which stitches match the textures; for example stitches that are fat at one end thin at the other, french knots that are round, bullion knots that are elongated. You are not trying to make an exact copy but your analysis will enable you to preserve the qualities of the textures. Now take a small area of a photograph and translate that into an area of stitches. Keep to one colour but different kinds and thicknesses of threads. If you think more than one stitch in the area is needed to make the effect then use them.

You can do rubbings of surfaces with wax crayons on thin typing paper and use sections of those to inspire you for a piece of stitchery. Some beads and shiny threads will add interest and make the experiment more like a little embroidery.

Throughout these experiments you should be looking at photographs for little things you would not have thought of on your own and trying to make your work more interesting. The more you look now the more you will be able to do on your own later when you can build up ideas and effects in your mind.

3. Looking at Shapes

A design for embroidery is made up of lines, shapes and textures, together with colour. After line you will need to study shapes and then put the two together.

In embroidery the shapes will be made with fabrics all of which have different surface textures and these will now form the main bulk and structure on which you build. You will have to be careful which dominates, line or shape.

In the same way that lines have a relationship with each other and with the outer edge, so do shapes, but this relationship seems to be emphasized because of the area of the shapes.

The essence of good embroidery is in design and it is important to try to get this well balanced before you begin stitching. 'Well balanced' does not mean symmetrical. You must continue the ideas from your line work, those of variation, uneven spacing and interest

Plant shapes   Man-made shapes

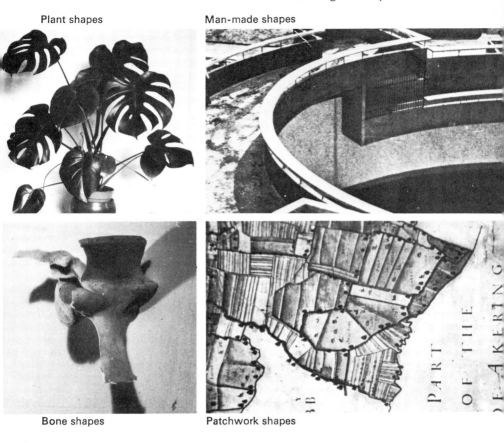

Bone shapes   Patchwork shapes

in grouping. For instance, one shape on one side can be balanced by two smaller ones on the other side.

You now have to look at the shapes (positive) and the space you are leaving (negative). This is often made more interesting when a shape goes off the outer edge. Shape and space are equally important. When you put a shape on your background you create a new space-shape with what you leave. Sometimes this negative space-shape looks positive because you have enclosed it with two or more shapes. This is what happens with 'op' art, which appears to move as you look at it. You are aiming at something well balanced, satisfying to look at, with pleasing composition, and so the negative/positive interchange is likely to take place only where your area of interest is. This is the focal area.

Simple panel inspired by the inside of a barn, designed and worked by
Mary Caroll in dark brown, yellow and golden yellow

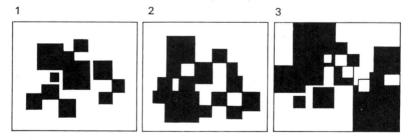

1. Relationship and pull between shapes
2. Negative/positive
3. Greater use of the spaces in between — the making of new shapes and a
   focal area

Remember that an area of interest must also have an area of plain to balance it. In order to understand how to 'balance' negative and positive areas you need to produce some simple designs. These are obviously abstract because they are so simple, but if you were doing a design based on flowers or trees the same principle would apply. Try these ideas:

1. Holding three square pieces of paper together, cut them into two shapes, with a square cut. Take one square at a time and arrange

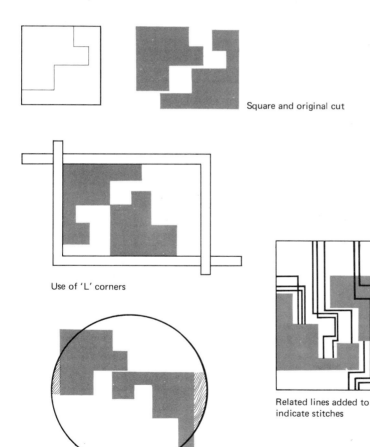

Square and original cut

Use of 'L' corners

Related lines added to indicate stitches

Extend the shapes where you wish

These arrangements are all from the same cut

the two shapes on a larger piece of paper. Then using two 'L' corners of paper move them so that you get a satisfactory composition and balance all shapes, negative and positive. Paste down the shapes and draw in the rectangle you have decided on. (Try three different arrangements.)

2. Repeat the above experiment but this time cut the squares with a curved cut. This means that you now have to look at the relationship of the curves and the straight edges as you put them down. Try and cut so that the two shapes are not equal. You will probably find the straight edges relating to the outside with the curves inside.

Two arrangements with two different cuts, showing related lines for stitchery

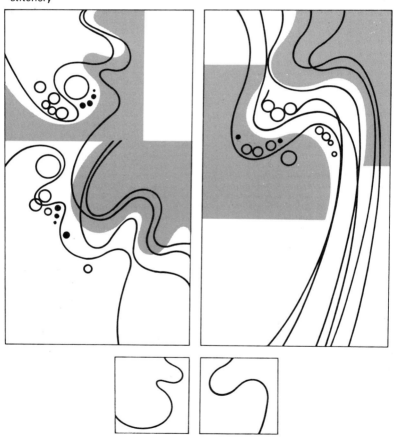

3. Take one of your experiments and place a sheet of tracing paper over it. Try adding related lines. These can go over and off the shapes or in between. Remember they are adding interest to the shapes. Decide which section you want to make important and draw the lines to lead you into and around that focal point. Bring these lines close to and away from the shapes.

The cut paper shapes represent fabric, and the lines indicate the stitches. So you have now designed an embroidery. When working such a piece you can add your own areas of interest such as knots, curtain rings or beads and enhance one as the focal point. These designs could be used for cushion covers, panels in a pinafore dress, panels to hang on the wall, or even the back of a waistcoat or the hem of some trousers. Whatever it turns into will determine your choice of fabric and method of working.

Getting more out of shapes – tone

Your work so far on paper may look rather simple but remember you have several surfaces of fabric, padding and stitchery, so a flat drawing suddenly takes on life because the shapes are now varied in intensity. This intensity is partly due to the 'tonal values' of the fabrics you are to use – the darkness or lightness of a colour.

You will have already found that darker colours differ in impact from lighter colours, for instance in the clothes you wear. This is visual, it 'seems' to happen.

A darker colour has more impact.
A darker colour seems to be closer.
A darker colour seems to be smaller than it actually is.

A lighter colour seems to be further away.
A lighter colour seems to expand in size.

You have to look at these apparent changes in relation to each other. A shape and its tonal values are going to be affected by those next to it.

If the tone of a shape is in contrast to most of its surrounding shapes, or if a shape is greatly contrasted with its neighbour, then these are the ones that show up first regardless of any other factors.

Tonal contrast is one of the most positive ways of creating your focal point or area.

Two bones showing that light on an object creates a natural tonal composition

It is therefore vital that you look at the design as a whole before sticking it on paper or finalizing it. You can keep changing tones in order to compare and then decide which one you like. If it looks right to you then that is the right one.

Try to develop this 'choosing' technique when you are comparing one way with another. You will begin then to choose the right one with very little trial and error. This technique must be employed with the embroidery as well, in choosing the right fabrics and threads. Nothing is fixed until you have chosen.

The arrangement of tone is almost the most important factor in a design. The colours may be interesting but they still have tonal values which must be right.

Taking this arrangement of squares, experiment as follows with black, white and two shades of grey papers:

1. on a black background;
2. on a white background;
3. on a grey background.

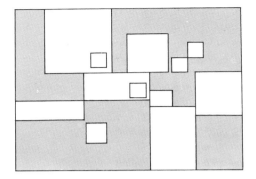

This will mean that you have to cut large and small squares in all papers so that you can use your choosing technique.

You will find that the difference in background completely changes your choice of tone and that it is easy to make different parts of the design stand out.

Look at what you have just done from a distance. Pin the three variations on a wall and stand back. Your three designs should now have taken on a three-dimensional appearance, whereas the design illustrated is totally flat.

Where is the focal point of each design? Can you decide why?

Can you see that your eyes have a tendency to link similar things together in that you notice the white shapes at the same time and then the black shapes together? Your eyes scan over others as they do this. So now you have to consider your tonal arrangement within a tonal arrangement. Try and make each tone flow through as though it were a stepping-stone path.

To go further with this, using colour, transfer the tonal work you have just done on paper to a fabric collage. You now have to find fabrics which match tonally the white-grey-black design on the paper. Sort out your fabrics, taking the full range from one set of colours (e.g. turquoise and bluey green ← GREEN → lime and yellowy green). When you have the appropriate pieces, cut out the squares and place them on the background, which must match exactly the tone (not the colour) of the paper. When you are satisfied that all are correctly placed, pin them on. Compare this pin-up with the pasted-paper design and see whether there are any differences in effect. If there are you must have the wrong tone in the fabrics. Make replacements and examine them again.

Now you have something in fabric you can see that the actual surface of the cloth makes quite a difference to the dominance of a shape.

Shiny shapes come forward: matt shapes go back.

Velvet and corduroy are dominant and heavy, tonally the darkest.

Gradually you have more to think about. If you enlarge the design, you can turn your collage into an embroidery by adding some lines at the drawing stage, and blocks of stitches and beads where you think your focal point is when you work it.

Applying shapes

From designing with shapes you now need to know how to handle them in fabric.

In general you should keep the weave of the shape matching the background fabric weave (grain). This is necessary for garments, practical pieces and anything which will stretch after applying in order to prevent wrinkles forming. It would be advisable to stick to this rule whenever possible. If you need to put a shape at an angle then 'iron on' stiffening on the wrong side will destroy the effect of the grain.

Sometimes you do not wish to draw attention to the outside edge of a shape. You may, for instance, just want a colour change and no line. At other times a line round the edge is part of the design and may even be in a contrasting colour; alternatively if a blurred edge is right then a hand-embroidered stitch over and beyond the edge is required. You must choose the method according to the design and the effect you want.

The various methods of appliqué are:

1. Stab-stitching by hand
2. Concealed method by hand
3. Over-card stitched by hand
4. Open zigzag on machine
5. Satin stitch on machine (closed zigzag)
6. Straight stitch on machine
7. Hand-stitching
8. Hand-stitching for blurred edges.

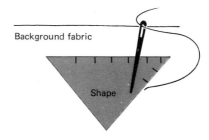

1. Stab-stitching by hand

This is used for leather and for fabrics which do not fray. The shape is cut to the exact size. Small stitches are worked in ordinary sewing thread with a fine needle at right angles to the edge. Bring the needle up through the fabric on the edge of the shape, stabbing down vertically into the shape. For leather and small shapes the stitches should be $\frac{1}{16}$ in./1·5 mm long and $\frac{1}{8}$ in./3 mm apart; for larger shapes they would be about $\frac{1}{4}$ in./6 mm apart. This is best worked when the background fabric is in a frame.

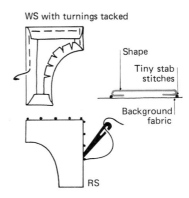

2. Concealed method by hand

This method involves cutting the shape larger to allow for a turning. Snip the edge if necessary and then press the turning to the wrong side. Pin and tack in position in the normal way, and then stab stitch to the background. Use very small stitches down the folded edge about $\frac{1}{4}$–$\frac{1}{2}$ in./6–12 mm apart. The stitches should be in matching thread and hardly visible. This is best worked when the background fabric is in a frame.

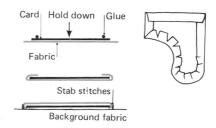

3. Over card

The card, which may vary in thickness from postcard to mounting card, is cut exactly to size. The fabric is cut with an extra $\frac{5}{8}$ in./16 mm to allow for turning. The fabric is stuck to the back of the card all round (probably using a PVC adhesive that dries clear), the turning being snipped where necessary. In order to avoid adhesive getting on the right side, keep the fabric flat on the table (right side down) and hold the card flat over that with the left hand while the right hand does the manoeuvring. Stick straight grains opposite first and then all round, gently pulling with the grain. This should prevent wrinkles from developing round the edge. Try to avoid picking it up until you have finally stuck down all round and wiped your hands. Stitch in place with tiny stab stitches every $\frac{1}{2}$ in./12 mm and matching thread; the background is stretched on or in a frame.

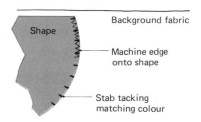

4. Open zigzag on machine

This method is employed before the work is stretched.

The shape is cut to size and stab-tacked using the stab stitches as in No. 1, only spacing them up to $\frac{1}{2}$ in./12 mm apart, with the colour you are to machine with. Leave the work flat on the table the whole time, using both hands to manipulate the needle. Keep flattening the shape as you work. This is the only way to ensure a good result.

This method of tacking is used in appliqué for two reasons: the stab stitches keep the shape in place better as the machine pushes over them, and they do not have to be removed after machining.

This method would be used for ribbons, insertions and braids that you wish to stitch on flat.

The zigzag stitch should be worked from the edge of the shape inwards and not half on, half off. This way it will be much firmer and less likely to pull away on the cross-grain.

The top tension should be slightly loosened so that the stitch is smooth on top, as wide as possible and as open as you wish: normally, your average stitch length.

Start with the needle on the RHS bringing it down through the fabric on the edge of the shape. Put the presser foot down and begin machining. It will naturally swing into the shape.

5. Satin stitch on machine (closed zigzag)

This is the same as No. 4 only your zigzag is close together. There is normally a red dot or some other mark to indicate this on the stitch-length regulator of your machine (used for buttonholes). The closeness will vary according to the thickness of the fabric being applied: the thinner the fabric, the closer you can get the stitch. Try the stitch first with the fabrics you want to use. This method is good for practical articles as it is flat and very durable.

A contrasting stitch colour might be interesting when using this method on clothes.

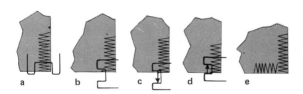

Coping with a corner.   Machine to the corner, stopping on the edge of the shape, with the needle on the left-hand side (inside) in the fabric.

Lift the presser foot and turn the corner.

Drop the presser foot down again (it will be seen that the foot is now off the shape).

Using the hand wheel, turn until the needle nearly goes into the fabric (away from the shape).

Lift the presser foot and bring the shape in line with the needle (on its edge).

Now continue down that side until you reach the next corner.

This ensures that the stitches do not overlap at the corner which is usually the cause of the stitch piling up.

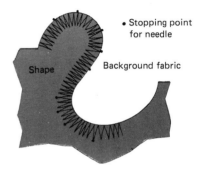

Coping with the curves. You are aiming at a continuous smooth line to your zigzag, which will mean tackling the curve in a series of small lengths, changing the angle as you go round. You must not try to pull the fabric round as you machine because this ends in puckering and stretching, and with the stitches at peculiar angles.

You will need to stop at regular intervals round the shape with the needle in the fabric, lifting the presser foot and moving the material freely round a little each time, working short lengths at a time. Stop with the needle on the outside of the shape for an outside curve and on the inside for an inside curve. This means that the zigzag slightly overlaps at an angle and does not leave a gap in the stitching.

6. Straight stitch on machine

An ordinary straight stitch on the machine can be used on the edge of a shape that does not fray (leather, PVC, jersey) or on the folded edge, like a patch, for other fabrics. For these you would cut the shape with turnings, press them to the wrong ·side and tack the shape in place.

Waistcoat in corduroy showing simple design in shapes applied on top like a patch

Machine close to the edge in matching thread and remove the tacking.

This is suitable for clothes and practical articles when you have no zigzag facility on your machine.

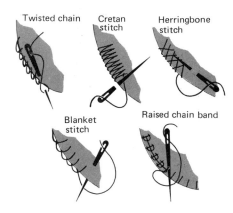

7. *Hand-stitching*

A shape can be applied with any hand-embroidery stitch which can be worked with some width to it, so that it will go over the edge and on to the shape.

It is advisable to stab tack the shape in place first, but it does not matter if the edges are raw.

Buttonhole stitch, herringbone, twisted chain, raised chain and cretan are the main stitches to try.

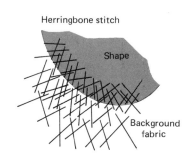

8. *Hand-stitching for blurred edges*

This involves repeating the stitch several times, overlapping and getting thinner or more open as it goes outwards from the shape. Buttonhole, cretan and herringbone stitch are ideal.

Scattered small shapes held down by free stitchery

Fabric glued over card and stitched together, then stab-stitched in position

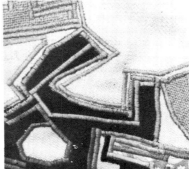

Stab-stitching of felt. Corduroy
with turning to wrong side

Satin stitch zigzag appliqué

4. Creating Relief

Relief is one of the most important qualities in embroidery. It is the essence of an embroidery and works well when used in moderation and in contrast to a flat or smooth area.

There are basically two kinds of relief, *smooth* (padded areas of fabric and flat fabric, over card) and *textured* (beads, stitches, ribbons and the like). This chapter deals with various ways of creating the two kinds of relief.

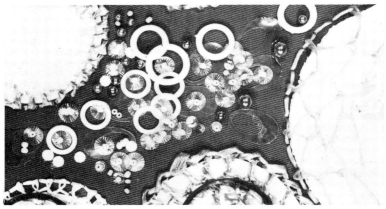

Two contrasting forms of relief – one plastic the other of threads

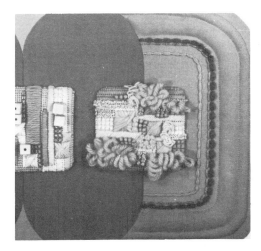

Slit on wrong side

Detail from panel using
an already printed
material worked by the
author. The quilting
relates to the canvaswork
shapes

Padded relief

Quilting and padding are basically the same thing.

(a) Quilting of the background fabric

Quilting is worked before stretching your background on to a frame.

A backing fabric is required (mentioned in the list of materials in Chapter 1). This needs to be a firm plain fabric, not too thick, such as plain cotton, cotton mixture, calico, curtain lining or poplin.

Your design should already be tacked on the background material.

If there are a lot of shapes to be padded cut the backing to the full size of the embroidery. If there are only one or two shapes, cut the backing to extend just beyond them, remembering it is underneath. The grain of the backing must match up with the background fabric.

Tack the backing and background fabrics together in several straight lines across the work.

Machine round the shapes.

Fasten off the ends securely by stitching them back down the line of machining on the wrong side.

Remove the tacking lines.

Stuff from the wrong side by cutting a slit in the backing fabric and pushing small pieces of wadding into the shape. It is important that every slit must follow the grain; any number can be cut in order to reach into awkward shapes.

The wadding is usually kapok, but tricel or terylene should be used when washing or dry-cleaning is required.

When the shape is firm enough stitch the slit up with a 'fishbone' stitch. This ensures the slit does not overlap and pull tighter than originally.

(b) Quilting appliquéd

The backing fabric is now your background material as you are putting another on top of that. Continue as (a), cutting a slit in the background fabric.

Padded shapes on card

Cut out exact shape of card.

Cut out the shape with allowances in a lining-type fabric. Lay this R S down on the table and pile on top of it some kapok or wadding.

Hold over that the card and stick the lining fabric to the card, keeping the stuffing inside.

You can now turn it over for examination. Restick any bits that might be too tight, too loose or pleated. It does not matter if adhesive gets on this part. It is practice for the top layer.

Now cut out the actual fabric for the shape (with turnings) and stick that over your pad.

Lay in place and stab-stitch every $\frac{1}{4}$ in./6 mm. These stitches are better worked when the background is stretched.

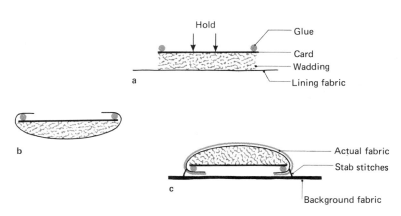

Hold
Glue
Card
Wadding
Lining fabric
a

b

Actual fabric
Stab stitches
Background fabric
c

Padded soft shapes (made like a pillow case)

Cut out two shapes of the same fabric, RS together, with turnings.
Machine round these leaving a small gap, on an easy side, of about
1–1½ in./25–38 mm.
Finish off ends of thread.
Snip the turnings on corners and curves and turn RS out.
Stuff and stitch up gap very carefully.
Lay in position on embroidery. Pin in place and stab stitch on
through seam line, pushing the underneath layer inside if it tends
to push outwards.

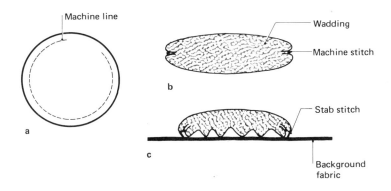

The shape may need initially to be a little bigger than the actual
one on your embroidery to allow pulling-in during stuffing.
It should be stitched on only when the background is stretched.

Flat-card shapes

This method just casts a shadow round the edge of the shape and
can be varied according to the thickness of the card.
See p. 50. Applying shapes over card.

Felt-padded shapes

This method is for small shapes up to 1½ in. 36 mm in one direction.
The background fabric must be stretched on a frame. The shape
is padded with layers of felt, starting with a small one in the
middle and then getting larger.

Each layer has to be eased over the pad being formed, as you stitch. The shape should be outlined with a tack on the background fabric.

In order to achieve a smooth even pad the following instructions must be followed:

1. The first layer of felt is cut about $\frac{1}{4}$ in./6 mm in size (not more than $\frac{1}{2}$ in./12 mm). Cut two if you want the pad to push up a little more.

2. Stitch in the centre of your tacked shape, top, bottom, and then the two sides, N.S.E.W. In other words, bring the needle through on the edge down into the shape.

3. The next layer is cut $\frac{1}{8}$ in./3 mm larger all round. Hold it on top of the previous layer and stab-stitch it down, 'N.S.E.W.' again. Then catch down in between each of those stitches, easing the felt as you go round.

4. Repeat No. 3 but put two stitches in between your original four if you think the spacing too great.

5. Repeat No. 4. Each time put a stitch in between the ones you have just done, so that the easing of the felt is perfectly even.

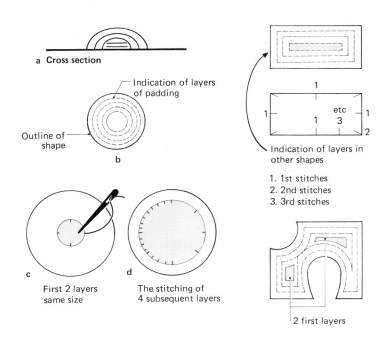

a Cross section

Indication of layers of padding

Outline of shape

b

1. 1st stitches
2. 2nd stitches
3. 3rd stitches

Indication of layers in other shapes

c   First 2 layers same size

d   The stitching of 4 subsequent layers

2 first layers

As the shape gets larger ease the felt down with your finger in order to see where the needle should come through the background fabric.

You should end with the stitches $\frac{1}{8}$ in./3 mm apart $\frac{1}{16}$ in./1·5 mm long and perfectly even.

6. Cut the last layer in leather and stab-stitch carefully with matching thread and a fine-pointed needle. A special leather needle is not necessary. Remember that these stitches will show.

For a square or angled shape stitch down the sides first and then bring in the corners to the right places.

For odd shapes you should cut each layer as you need it, laying it over the pad each time to check. The more height you build up, the more it alters the outline of the shape you need to cut. You cannot cut them all out before you start.

Textured relief

The creation of relief in other ways is linked with stitches and various threads. Here are some ideas and then you can experiment further. See also Texture stitches, p. 38.

Try couching four or five threads together, pulling the bunch up into loops as you work each couching stitch in an ordinary machine thread. Hold the stitch firm as you do the next. This should be done on a frame.

Detail from panel by the author

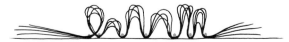

Detail from panel by the author

Ribbon can be looped or pleated as you stitch it on. Using matching machine thread, take a small stab-stitch from side to side of the ribbon guiding it into a curve if you need to. The loop (or humps) in the ribbon should then radiate on the curves.

Curtain rings with buttonhole stitch worked round them are good for areas of isolated interest. They blend well with beads. The buttonhole stitch is worked before the ring is applied.

The needle comes –
'Up through the ring (then),
Up through the loop.'

This creates a knotted ridge on the outer edge which looks particularly good with raffia or a shiny thread.

Try rolling up strips of felt to use on their ends. Experiment with different widths and lengths of each strip. Catch down the end of the felt as invisibly as possible, and stitch them either sideways or end up which would give more relief.

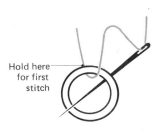

Hold here
for first
stitch

Hanging worked on a printed
fabric — joined together first.
The embroidery relates to the
print in colour and form. Worked
by the author

Detail from panel by Yvonne Robbins

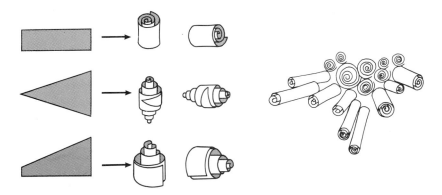

Detail from panel by Margaret Marklew. The macramé forms a relief in which beads and stitchery, ribbons and threads have been used

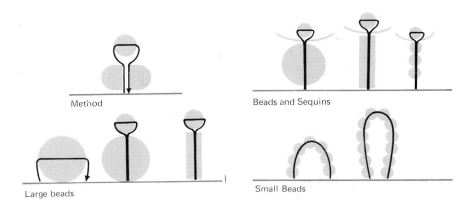

Method

Large beads

Beads and Sequins

Small Beads

Beads as a contrast to quilting

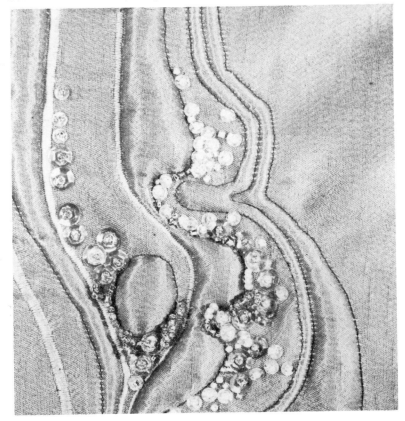

If you have some cords they are good to couch flat or pleat as you would ribbons. In firm thicker threads this would create considerable relief.

Beads automatically create interest as they are normally made of materials like glass, wood or plastic, which are very different from fabric and thread. Because of their size and surface they cast the little shadows needed for relief.

Beads can be sewn on in various ways so that they stick up from the background fabric. Try them out, varying the size and height, combining shiny glass with wood and so on.

You now have more idea about how you can create an area of interest in an embroidery.

To enlarge a design

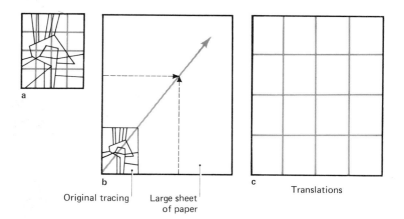

a

b

Original tracing

Large sheet
of paper

c

Translations

Trace your design and make sure you have the outer edge as well.

Place this tracing in the corner of another piece of paper large enough for the full size. Draw a diagonal line across your original and on to the large sheet. (You will find it helpful, but not essential, to use graph paper for this.)

Any line taken vertical or horizontally to meet on this diagonal will give you an enlarged, equally proportioned, rectangle. If you know you want something 18 in. across or, say, 50 cm, take the ruler up until the correct measure mark touches the diagonal and then draw the vertical.

Remove your original. With another colour divide it into four sections in both directions (by folding is the easiest) and subdivide areas which are complicated. If the design is complicated all over, divide it into six or eight.

Divide your large version in the same way and subdivide the same areas.

Translate what happens in the small rectangles on to the large ones, faintly in pencil.

First look for the obvious bits in the design: see if any lines touch the grid, or go into any corners, and mark those. Mark any lines that cross the grid in the middle, say a third or a quarter of the measure from the edge. Are any lines parallel? Look at the curves in relation to the straight lines. Gradually you can join up and complete it.

Review the drawing and redraw any curves which do not look quite right in the enlarged version.

When you are satisfied go over the enlarged design with a fine felt pen. Keep this for reference. The grid lines can serve as straight grain lines for fabrics. Make another tracing of this with a felt pen to use for transferring the design.

Transferring the design

The method used for most purposes and on all ordinary fabrics is that of tacking the design.

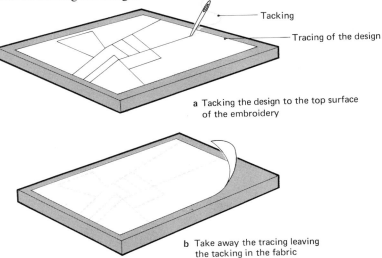

Tacking

Tracing of the design

a Tacking the design to the top surface of the embroidery

b Take away the tracing leaving the tacking in the fabric

Pin the tracing on to the background fabric and tack with a colour not too different from the background colour. Use small stitches about $\frac{1}{4}$ in./6 mm, fastening off carefully when you have to. Try to work flat on the table without picking up the fabric.

Tack the outer limit as well.

When complete, tear off the tracing paper and you are left with the design on the fabric.

Further ideas for a design

Now try doing an embroidery which you can develop further and instead of cutting up paper for shapes try retracing a drawn shape. Think of something simple like a leaf, a piece of fruit, or a bottle. Draw the shape and then, using tracing paper, repeat it by moving the tracing paper and redrawing whole or parts of the shape as they overlap. If it looks too much when you have finished, retrace the whole thing leaving out fussy or complicated parts, then add your own related lines where you want them.

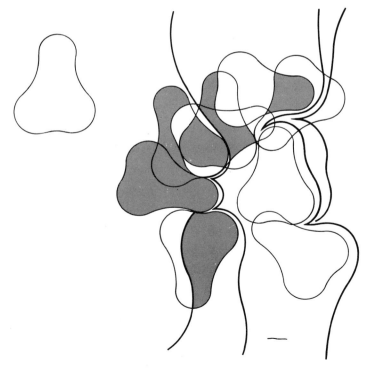

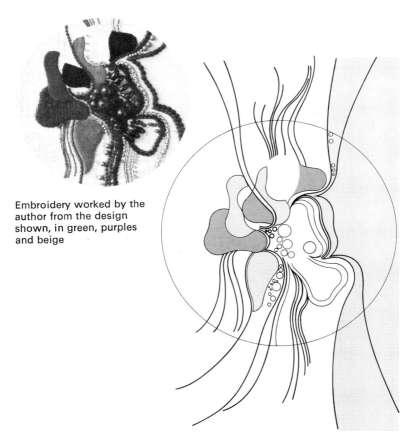

Embroidery worked by the
author from the design
shown, in green, purples
and beige

You now have to decide which shapes are applied, and therefore
change colour, and which can be padded. For some both processes
may be suitable. You must decide which lines are to be thick threads
and how they are to be linked with the colour of the shapes; which
lines are in the same colour as the background and therefore stand
out less; and finally where you are going to put your centre of
interest.

If you still do not feel confident enough to work a design of your
own, find a bold furnishing fabric and use a section from it. There
are also some tea towels on the market with good simple designs.
You can follow the shapes provided and emphasize with thicker
stitches and textures the sections you like, leaving some plain areas.
The character of the print will determine the choice of stitches.

5. Colour

Colour is not a static quality: it appears to change. Reactions are visual and depend on position. In other words, things seem to happen to colours when you put them in position. You must have tried on a garment and decided you looked wrong in it and possibly said that it drained you of any colour you originally had. Try to observe what happens to colours when you put them together. Sometimes a shape seems to be drained of its colour, enhanced, reduced in size or enlarged, when a contrasting colour is put next to it; or it can appear to come forward or be further away.

For instance if you placed a green square on a larger white one and another on a black one and repeated that with yellow you will find that the green seems larger on the black than on the white and the opposite appears to be so for the yellow. If you put your green on to a grey square the grey appears pinky and warm looking, if you do the same with the yellow then the grey seems darker and bluer, especially where the two touch each other. A more neutral colour like grey always seems to take on the complementary of the one on it or next to it. This is called 'simultaneous contrast'. A complementary colour is that which is opposite another on the colour circle on the facing page.

Colours also appear to have weight and energy. The amount of power a colour has is also affected by its neighbours. They might lower its value, or alternatively give it more if they happen to be the complementary; as all complementaries heighten each other.

You are lucky as an embroiderer as you can choose and look at the result of putting certain pieces of fabric together before you carry out the work.

Now look at the colour circle:

Directions for compiling a colour circle

The three primaries must be very carefully chosen, so that they appear exactly in between their adjacent ones. Yellow must be a 'pure yellow' not slightly 'buttery' (orange/yellow) or slightly 'lemony' (green/yellow); it must be exactly in between the two. The

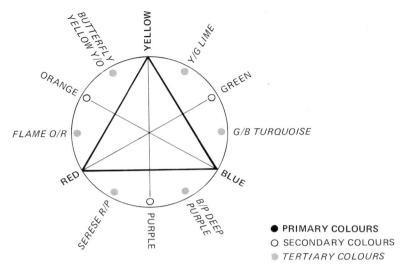

● PRIMARY COLOURS
○ SECONDARY COLOURS
◗ TERTIARY COLOURS

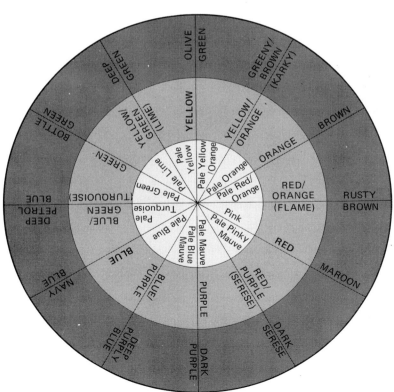

same with red and blue. Similarly the secondary and tertiary colours should fit exactly in between their neighbours.

When each colour has thus been chosen the circle should have the same intensity and pureness of colour for each one (nothing must look as though it has white with it). Then you can glue them in place.

Next imagine what those colours would be mixed with white (tints) and place them on the outer circle. They should all 'read' as having an equal amount of white in each. Glue when you are sure.

Repeat this process with the shades, they should all appear to be equally dark. Some colours change more when black is added.

Greens, blues and purples all seem similar only much darker; reds turn into 'plums' and maroons, orange into rich brown; yellow/orange into less warm brown; yellow into olive green and lime green into a greener olive. These should show a gradual progression as you view the whole circle and by looking at this circle you can see the complementary colours straight away by following the lines across the circle.

Colour schemes

One of the most important factors in your design is the tonal values of the colours you use.

Think in blacks, greys and whites first and then transpose them into colours that fit your scheme you have chosen.

If you cannot see colours as dark and light while you are arranging them, then it is best at first to do all your work using paper in greys and so on, from newspapers, magazines and photographs. It should not look 'jumpy' or 'bitty' but contain some control in the use of your tones, especially the arrangement of the blacks and whites, as these stand out most.

Having got the tones right arrange small pieces of fabric over your tracing or design so as to see what sort of impact they have and if the focal area is achieved satisfactorily.

There are several ways in which you can devise colour schemes. You should try all of these for yourself so that you have something positive to look at, choose from and criticize. You need to see things and make choices. Some people have very strong preferences, others can go from using very pale, soft colours to bright red and green and then blacks and browns. It is often the nature of a piece which determines the colour scheme or it may just be the way you are feeling at the time.

Colour schemes can be found in your surroundings either in nature (birds, butterflies or flowers), or in man-made objects (printed materials, a page in a magazine or an advertisement). Keep looking and collecting photographs for this purpose.

It is not only the colours and their tonal values but the amount (area) of each colour which is important.

The greater the number of pure colours the more they seem to conflict with each other unless their areas are considered very carefully.

Mixing colours with equal amounts of cold and warm values results in a dead mixture and the temperatures cancel out; equal amounts of complementary ranges result in an unresolved fight.

By the use of contrasts and varying the amounts of colours used you can achieve a colour scheme which is good to look at and spatially interesting. The balance in an area is not equal, blue needs a greater amount of orange, and yellow needs a much smaller amount of purple to create a satisfactory equilibrium.

As in line and shape, the use of contrasts creates the focal area – either warm/cold, light/dark, complementary contrast, contrast in proportion, or the contrast in the degree of saturation (pure colours with 'dirty' mixed colours).

Your eye links similar colours together when viewing an embroidery. You will notice all reds, all greens, all the very dark colours or all the very light colours together. So a colour must have a good relationship with itself as well as the whole design.

Using your colour circle for colour schemes

Decide on a main colour you would like to use and look at it on the circle and at its immediate neighbours so that you have a complete family of colours (say three or four next to each other).

If you use just these then you would achieve something quite 'safe' and harmonious. Remember that though you have the whole range from very light to very dark and different amounts of them all, in fact you would not use them all, you would use those in that range that you liked. The interest would be in using contrasting tones as the colours will probably not vary a great deal (because they are adjacent on the circle).

If you like dark rich colours then use mostly those and only small amounts of the lighter brighter colours.

Alternatively you can make a soft quiet scheme by using the paler ones with only touches of dark where the design requires it.

This family-type scheme is good when you include something from the complementary range. This may be only a shade of that colour giving the dark colours a bit of life.

Developing this idea further by seeing whether you like black, white or grey in the scheme, or possibly the beige types of neutral colours. White makes things brighter and richer, and black lightens the colours. It is up to you to decide whether it will suit your embroidery.

Close your eyes and think of two complementary colours, say yellow and purple. Your first thoughts are of a bright warm yellow and a deep rich purple. These are the hues, the saturated colours. Now think of the shades and tints. Yellow, you think of as light, purple dark. Reverse this – dark yellow (olive green) and light purple (soft flowery mauve). These are far more interesting and subtle.

Now you could use several dark olives, greens and even going to browns with touches of mauve, and pinky mauve if you like. Alternatively, reverse the quantities – several mauves with touches of olive/muddy greens.

Repeat the same idea with other complementary colours.

Use the full range of tones and hues from one side of the circle, but put with them either the light or dark version of the complementary (not the normal hue) – say pinks, reds and maroons with bottle green.

Now try an idea in fabrics. Take two complementary colours. Decide which you prefer and select scraps of fabric to fit within the close range of that and its near neighbours (hues, shades and tints). Add one or two tones of the complementary. Here you have no idea of the amounts you want.

Decide on your background colour. Will it be one of the complementary colours? Dark or light?

Now start with varying sizes of fabric pieces, laying them on the background colour. Move them round. You will find some colours look better near others and not necessarily where you might think. Watch the size of each patch of colour. Sometimes use more than one piece of a particular colour.

Do you use all you had collected or just three or four with small touches of the complementary?

Where have you put your complementary colour or colours?

Have you put both the dark and light of your complementary?

Stand back and see if anything stands out more than you want it to. Try replacing it and criticize again. Watch the change in tone and avoid a chequerboard effect.

Look at the relationship of one colour in its various positions, does it appear to jump about too much?

You are now able to use those colours, those amounts and wherever possible those positions of colour – or at least colours you have next to each other – in an embroidery.

Look at three equally spaced colours, say orange/purple/green, and take the light of two with the dark of the third, or alternatively the darker of two with the light of the third. This is a 'triad' colour scheme. You always need to experiment with scraps of coloured fabrics in order to see the amounts and positions of a scheme. What will the background colour be?

You could now continue to take some ideas from elsewhere by observation and recording and then using those as schemes.

Take a flower or a butterfly or any natural object you like for its colour – if possible the actual thing – and look at it carefully.

What colours are in it? Are there many shades of one colour?

Now cut $\frac{1}{2}$ in./12 mm squares of fabric in these colours and stick them on to card, starting in the middle, to make a mosaic of the object.

If necessary cut some squares in half if a smaller proportion is required and use several of the same colour if more is required. The idea is to get the right positions of colour and the right amounts.

Check that no colour stands out more than it should. This has now made more impact on you and you can decide if any colours seem to you to be in the wrong place.

The proportions and positions could now be used in an embroidery The background colour could be something completely different but it is more likely to be one of the main colours. Try repeating this idea with another subject – from a painting you like.

It is a good idea to study how other people have used colour. You will begin to understand the importance of the positions of colours over the whole piece. Modern paintings and old masters are worth studying so that you can see what your preferences are.

Look at printed fabrics, especially some of the modern furnishing fabrics, to analyse whether their colour scheme falls into a pattern or not, for example, whether complementary colours are dominant, triad, and so on.

Have they got white or black in? If so do you think that helps?

If you were going to use those colours for an embroidery would you put white in?

Even if you decide on a colour scheme by picking up a bundle of pieces which happen to look good on the table, you still have to decide on the amounts of each in order to get the balance, and on the background colour. All this is trial and error in collage form.

6. Designing for Practical Embroidery

Your approach to a practical design would be exactly the same as for a panel. The only difference is in the shape of the background. A cushion cover or teapot cosy might be circular or semicircular and a waistcoat has armholes. You have also the three-dimensional qualities to consider, as the article is viewed from different angles.

There are more considerations though, for articles that are to be worn or used, and will need washing or dry-cleaning.

Is the background material suitable for the purpose. Will it shrink if washed or should it be dry-cleaned? Is the weave firm enough?

Are the threads washable if the background is?

Where is the article to go?

What colour scheme will go with those surroundings?

Where is the article to be handled, picked up or rubbed if worn?

Should a means of holding (handle, knob, loop, flap, etc.) be incorporated in the design?

From which angle will it be looked at and therefore what area will be seen? Has the design to be considered all round something? Or, will it be seen mainly on one side as, for example, in trousers.

Is the technique you envisage durable enough? You cannot be quite so free in your embroidery when there are practical considerations.

Points to remember

* Ribbons (except nylon) need washing before they are used in embroidery.

Three uses of hand embroidered
lines, mostly chain, double-knot
stitch and couching as decoration for
clothes

* Use firm threads which do not stretch. As you are likely to be working without a frame, tensioning will be difficult.
* Mix threads, but if they may be washed make sure they are washable.
* Use tricel acrylic filling for padded areas. Kapok does not wash.
* Use the wide, close zigzag for appliqué, or fold the raw edge under and use a straight stitch, as with a patch.
* The grain of the shapes must follow the background grain.
* If the article is to be handled a lot stitch beads on with nylon thread and secure on the back with iron-on stiffening.
* Stitches must not be longer than $\frac{1}{2}$ in./12 mm or they will catch and pull.
* Start and finish securely, being careful about knots because they create bulk.
* Never use felt as it has no weave and will not wash or dry-clean.
* Individually padded shapes (trapunto quilting) are not good on something that is to hang freely because it tends to pucker round the edge.

Practical designs

At first you can use the simple methods of design shown at the beginning of the book. Designs will have to be adapted to suit practical needs. Look for interesting fabrics and keep texture solidly held in place. Often a range of one colour will be more pleasing than a mixture of different colours. Later you will be able to progress to the ideas further on in the book.

Preliminary make-up

Consider whether any seams, darts or joining of pieces should be done before you begin the embroidery: waistcoat or skirt side seams for instance. It is as well to leave the centre back or centre front of a skirt, or shoulder seams of a jacket or waistcoat open to work flat and to allow a little more fabric in case some is used up. For hand embroidery it will only be a small amount. If you like the idea of borders, consider the width of border in relation to the rest, the closeness to the edge, and the relationship the design has with the edge: it might have a straight line near the edge and a curved free line on the inner edge. Shapes might end level towards the bottom

Above: Border designed from simple cut shapes interpreted into machine appliqué, ribbon and hand embroidery. Designed and worked by Helen Woolmer

Above right: Border on a long black evening skirt in purple. Designed and worked by the author using lines of velvet ribbon, hand embroidery and machine stitchery

Right: Detail of this border

edge and extend to different levels upwards. Can the border turn a corner or curve if it has to? It would be best to try your ideas on paper the size you think you might work.

Now look at your border in trial form in either paper and threads, or fabric and threads. Are the lines too even? Are the spaces interesting? Are there too many different shapes together? Where is the weight in the design? Is it where you want it to be?

It is advisable with clothes to pin shapes in place and to look at the result in a mirror. Hold the garment up to you to see what the balance is like in colour and tone. You do not want your eyes to be drawn to the wrong parts of your body.

The complexity in the design will probably depend on how much time you have to work it.

Fabric boxes

A square box can be made with any thick, firm, good-quality card, but even that tends to break up on the corners if it is roughly handled. The proper card is called 'millboard', and is black and carefully made in layers so that it can be bent into a round box. Only 'millboard' can be used for a round box, everything else cracks. You will need some ordinary thin card as well, strong sewing cotton, a firm long needle, not too thick, and a small curved needle if you can get it. Other equipment: adhesive for sticking fabric to card, a Stanley cutting knife and a ruler for cutting out the card; synthetic wadding for padding the lining if you wish (a thin foam sheet serves the same purpose)—millboard from Dryad Ltd.

The size of a hand-made box should not be too big, as the sides tend to curve outwards. Putting panels inside to divide it up and support the sides is much more difficult. Up to 8 in./20 cm on a square or long side of a rectangle would be advisable at this stage.

The fabric for the outside should be strong, closely woven and all in one colour, not a fabric with the weave having one colour one way and another the other way – these will show stitch pull marks when sewn, and so will very shiny fabrics. Such materials as dralon, furnishing fabrics, heavy cottons, corduroys and dress wools are good. For the lining you need something thinner and softer, such as jersey, Viyella, dress crêpe and cotton. If you wish to pad the inside the synthetic jersey fabrics are ideal. It is best to avoid a shiny satin

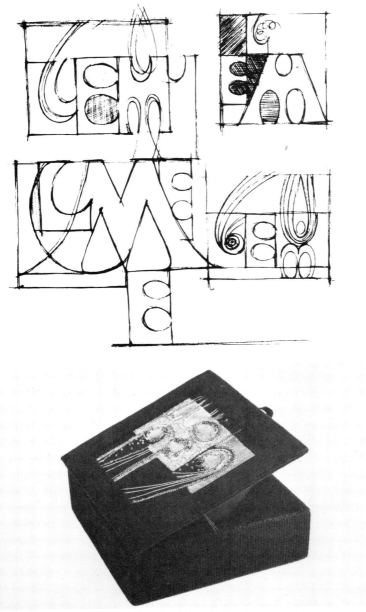

Brown corduroy box with gold embroidery designed as a birthday present
by the author

as this shows stitch pull marks and ordinary lining material is much too thin, and not strong enough when stretched over the card.

It is sometimes a good idea to fold a strip of paper to reproduce the size of the box you are thinking of making, and see if its proportions are right. It might be too deep, or you might like more depth to embroider round the sides.

Make the base up first and then check the measurement for the lid, as it is usually fractionally bigger than the base. The embroidery will then look right and reach fully to the extent you require.

A square box is made from the inside out and a round one from the outside in. The lid can be lifted off separately or it can be hinged at the back of the box. If it is to be lifted then the means of lifting must be incorporated in the centre of the design on the lid, such things as a large bead, loop of ribbon, tassel or a loop of beads could be used, the design working round this central point.

If you are going to hinge the box the design can be of any form as the means of lifting the lid is placed on the outer edge at the front and hangs down so as not to detract from the design on the top.

The hinges have to be put in while making up, so you must make this decision early on.

To make a square or rectangular box

1. Using the card, measure and draw the base and sides accurately. Check the right-angles otherwise the box will not have straight sides.

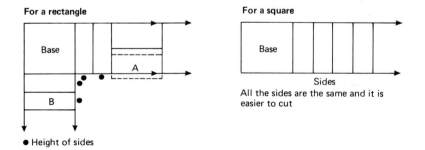

(b) is better as you continue the cut already needed for the base.

(a) if the height is more than half the short side of the box then the sides will stick out as shown in the diagram.

These are cut with the Stanley knife to get a sharp, clean, straight edge.

2. Cut pieces for the lining with a $\frac{5}{8}$ in./16 mm turning and have enough material for another piece the size of the base to go inside the lid.

Stick these to the card keeping the weave of the fabric level with the edges of the card (apply adhesive only on the back for the turnings) and not on the right side.

Keep the corners as neat and flat as possible, keeping the adhesive away from the edge of the card.

Methods A and B illustrated are suitable for the lining. B is easier.

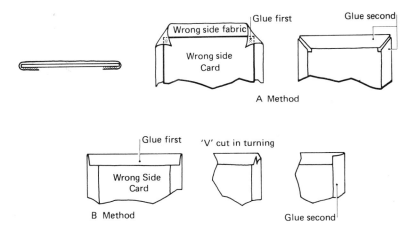

A Method

B Method

If you wish to pad each section, cut a piece of wadding or foam $\frac{1}{16}$ in./1·5 mm smaller all round than the card. With one or two spots of adhesive keep it in place on the card – do not press where the adhesive is until it has dried or the wadding will dent. Now cover over the wadding to the back of the card.

Edges and corners must be firm and neat, with no loose or limp sections.

3. The sides are stitched with small oversewing stitches round the base. Put the right sides together and using strong sewing cotton

pick up tiny bits of fabric on the very edge of each section, making stitches no more than $\frac{1}{8}$ in./3 mm apart. When all four sides are on it should look like the diagram when laid flat.

4. Now lift up two sides and stitch down the corner from the top of the box to the base. If you work this way you will always keep the top level. You should now have a neat inside with the stuck down edges etc. on the outside.

5. Cut a strip of the material you are using for the outside approximately 1 in./2·5 cm wider than the height of your box and enough to wrap round with two seam allowances. Wrap it round the box and pin the seam. Machine and press flat. Cut off the corners on the turnings.

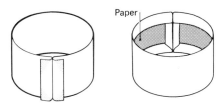

6. Fold to the wrong side a good $\frac{1}{2}$ in./12 mm of the top edge and press all round. Turn this so that the turnings are all on the inside and slide the strip from the base of the box up over it until the folded edge of the strip is level with the top of the box.

The seam must be in the middle of the back of the box.

If there is an impression of these turnings and the glued bits on the card, a strip of stiff paper is needed to disguise it. Cut this the height of the box and long enough to go all round and meet.

Now remove your outer piece and slide this paper strip under the folded top edge and under the seam that joins the strip.

Slide carefully back over the box.

7(a) Pin the top edge with pins vertically. This has either to be stitched with a very carefully disguised straight oversew in matching thread or with a decorative stitch. [If a hinge is required, now read 7(b).] It is better to have a decorative stitch that is meant to show than a bad one that is not meant to show. Twisted-chain, couching with a thicker thread or two thin ones, raised-chain band and even cross-stitch in a thicker thread look good. Perlé No. 5, buttonhole twist, and coton à broder are about the right thickness of thread.

7(b) If a hinge is required this must be put in place before you stitch the outside fabric to the box. The simplest and easiest form of hinge is made with strips of matching ribbon.

Cut three or four lengths of 1 in./2·5 cm or so. Tuck these in between the box and outside fabric and stitch in place at the same time as the fabric, one at either end and as many as necessary between. Later the other ends are to be stitched to the lid, now continue as in 7(a).

If this seems too difficult you can make buttonhole-stitched hinges right at the end when everything is made up, rather like the loop made in dressmaking for a hook instead of the eye provided.

8. Fold the side fabric round on to the bottom of the box and glue in place, following method 2(a) for the corners, which should be mitred.

9. Cut a piece of card (not necessarily millboard), a little smaller than the base. Cover this with outside fabric, and then fix it in position on the bottom with whatever adhesive you are using.

It is likely you will find difficulty with the corners so these could now be stitched. Slant the needle across the corner starting as far back as you can for the length of needle and work your way towards the corner, catching down the base each time you take a stitch.

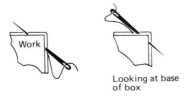

Looking at base
of box

10. Now cut your millboard for the lid, making sure it will just cover the box and not stick out too much. String your embroidery over it so that you can position it more accurately (see also Mounting, page 108). Pad the top if you wish in the same way as the inside.

Mitre the corners as the lining does not reach the outer edge of the lid (see 2a). Stitch on a loop for lifting the lid if it is to be ribbon or something similar at the front edge.

11. Pin the hinges in place if it is hinged, so that the lid will open, but check that they are not too loose when the lid is down. Stitch them to the lid $\frac{1}{4}$ in./6 mm in, so that the lining will cover the stitches.

12. Cut a piece of card so that it will drop into the top of the box. This is to go under the lid which must lie flat – therefore the lining must sit inside the box. Cover this with the lining and pad if you wish. This has to be stitched very carefully to the inside of the lid, and is tricky if the lid is held in place with hinges. Use the same decorative stitch as on the top edge of the box if you do not have a curved needle. Alternatively, stick with adhesive and stitch the corners as on the base (see 9).

To make a round box, using millboard

The information on fabrics and so on for the square box applies to the round one also.

1. Cut a circle of board for the base. A sharp, strong pair of scissors will give the best result. Sandpaper the edge to smooth off the roughness. Cover this with the outside fabric, either by stringing or with adhesive.

2. Cut a strip of board so that it will go round this circle, over-lapping a good inch (2·5 cm), by the height of the box.

The two overlapping edges have to be tapered so that they lie flat when overlapped and glued.

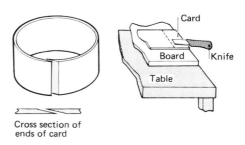

Cross section of
ends of card

This tapering is on the inside of one end and the outside of the other: draw the overlapping line on both and mark the side to be tapered.

Place the end of the strip, tapering side up, on the edge of a board which is itself on the edge of a table. Hold the Stanley knife at an angle and scrape away the card, working from the drawn line towards each corner and the edge, cutting some away on the edge, and ending up with a smooth taper. If you work diagonally towards each corner you do not cut into the card so much: you are half scraping and half cutting away, but not digging into the card.

Scraping action diagonally over the end of the card

You should end up with one thin layer of card on the very end.

Do both ends and then check what they are like when you overlap them. They must not bulge; if they do, scrape off some more card.
3. When you are satisfied, check this overlap round the base, make it fractionally loose as it is to be covered in fabric, and re-mark if necessary.

These two rough edges can now be stuck together; hold them in place with two paper clips or clothes pegs, then wait until the join is thoroughly dry forming your cylinder.
4. Cut a strip of outside fabric to wrap round the millboard cylinder plus two turnings, and $1\frac{1}{4}$ in./3 cm wider. Pin round the board and then machine and press the seam. Cut off the corners of the seam turnings. Turn to inside.
5. Slide this over the cylinder so that the seam is just to one side of the join in the card.
6. Turn the top margin of fabric ($\frac{5}{8}$ in./16 mm) over to the inside and stick down making sure the adhesive is no closer than $\frac{1}{4}$ in./6 mm from the top.
7. Do the same at the bottom edge.
8. You now have to stitch the base to the cylinder. The base should push inside the cylinder, and may need catching with a stitch in four places to hold it.

9. To stitch them together you have to work each stitch from the inside of the box through to the outside or vice versa, which is more difficult than when making a square box. Make the stitches as invisible as possible. If you want one hinge at the back, stitch a piece of ribbon to the top edge where the seam comes on the outside fabric as in the square box.

10. Cut a strip of thin card or thick paper for the lining; this should sit inside and just meet, not quite reaching the top edge.

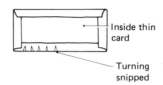

Inside thin card

Turning snipped

Cover this with lining cut larger. Stick the two ends first slightly stretching the material (as it is to be curved inwards), then the top edge.

11. Snip the bottom turning about every $\frac{1}{2}$ in./12 mm but do not stick.

12. Curve this round and place inside the box with the joint *opposite* the joint of the outside fabric. It should just touch and not overlap.

13. This lining has to be stuck in place by easing sections away from the side, carefully placing adhesive on the box or the lining and pushing it back, working your way round the lining as you go and then down the join.

14. The snipped lower edge has to be eased down and stuck to the bottom of the box as carefully as possible, trying not to get adhesive on the sides.

Hinge here if you wish

The joint in the lining will not be seen as this is the front of the box and you look past it into the box.

15. A circle of card covered in lining fabric must now be cut to drop into the box. It is fixed in place with adhesive.

16. The lid is finished in the same way as for the square box. A quilted or padded lining to the base and lid looks good; check that the lining to the lid sits in the box. It can be put on a thicker card to make sure of holding the lid in place.

7. Further Developments in Design

Design – a summary and check list

I have dealt with the main aspects of design separately but you must of course, become used to thinking of them all simultaneously.

The various aspects will get more instinctive or unconscious as you do more work, but here we should perhaps look at a check list as a reminder. Remember *you* have to enjoy looking at it.

Your order of working should be:
1. Shapes, 2. Lines. 3. Background shape (outside edge) that fits into a rectangle, circle, cushion or waistcoat shape. 4. Tonal values. 5. Texture. 6. Colour.

At about stage 3 you could think about the type of embroidery, the size and the purpose, as these might influence your decisions for 4, 5 and 6.

The design should look as though it has been thought out carefully and the shapes not just thrown together.

The shapes must 'balance' within the outside edge, some going off the edge to support the others and make the background more interesting.

The lines must work with the shapes and only go against them where you *want* discord. Watch where the thick ones go – lines that go right off the edge are good and tend to lead your eye in rather than out.

The tonal values (lights and darks) should be planned next and later translated into colour.

There must be a focal area, and this must be decided on before you develop texture and colour. What form of contrast will you use for it: line, size of shapes, tonal, colour or textural? In some way

Modern collage of letters

a part of your work must show up and probably look more interesting than the rest. It is likely to be the most 'worked' section too.

There must be some plain pieces of fabric left to show up the embroidery; these should not be central. At the same time you do not want a chequerboard effect in the tone, texture or colour, as it is unsettling to look at, unless the design has been based on the idea of interchange.

You do not want to distribute textures evenly, either stitched or the weaves of fabric, as this creates an all over boring appearance. Make sure some smooth very plain areas allow the texture to take on more significance. Such ideas as texture at the top getting smoother towards the bottom of something, say a hanging or jacket, or from the inside smoother all round to the outside, say for a cushion cover.

Now you can try some other ideas on design.

Using letters

Until you feel quite confident to draw them you must find your forms from your surroundings.

Letters have very interesting shapes, with a good combination of curved and straight edges, so that when used you will produce shapes and forms that link and that you would not have been able to think of on your own. They can be used in abstract or in monogram form when the latter is to be read and have some meaning for the embroiderer or the receiver. It will still be a design with the shapes carefully considered. Look back at the section on shapes, arranging them and consideration of the background area. Apply those ideas to your arrangements of letters.

Letters can be put in lines for borders of skirts, belts or curtains. Or used as an all-over design for a cushion cover or a jacket. One letter looks just as good as two, three or four. Certain considerations still apply. Where have you placed the letter(s) in relation to the background shape? How will you relate the lines to this?

You can now decide whether it turns into appliqué and stitches, quilting, quilting and stitches, or padded leather and couched threads. It will depend on the size you intend working it, and the purpose for which it is to be used.

In something simple like a skirt you need to arrange the letters with the spaces between and then see if you are going to apply only the letters, only the spaces or both.

Collage of letters from old manuscripts

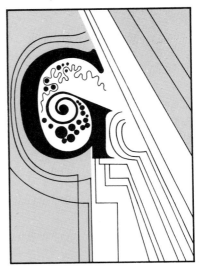

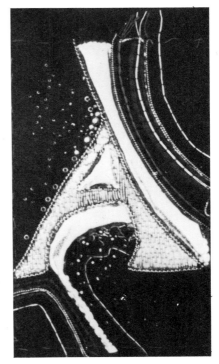

Small panel for a box top by Ann
Ralphs using the same method for
the design

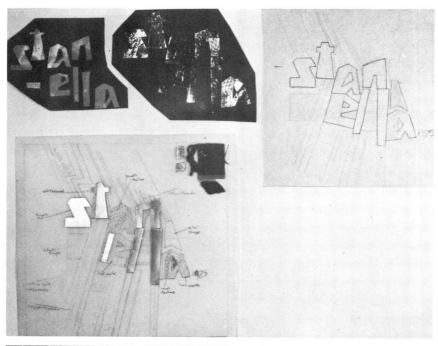

Design in progress

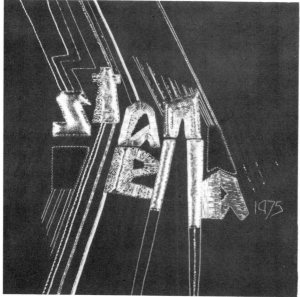

Embroidered panel in
gold by Dorothy
Barrowman who
designed it as a gift for
Stan and Ella

Now try letters plus lines.

Start by drawing a letter in the middle of a piece of paper, or cutting one out in paper. Using your 'L' corners again decide where you want to draw in your background.

Now cover this with tracing paper and play with lines. The lines must relate to the letter and some would go off the edge as a means of 'holding the letter down'. Watch the spacing of your lines, bring them close and then away, even overlap them.

If you use sticky paper your shape is defined but if you draw it then you can shade in shapes as you wish which will take the design further away from the letter you began with.

You can work in this way with any number of letters. Always use tracing paper over your basic arrangements so that you can try several ideas and choose the one you like. Use the same procedure for shading in shapes. If you try rubbing out or drawing on your original you are likely to spoil it and be unable to make up your mind. With tracing paper you can make any number of attempts.

You could try drawing one large letter and then retracing it three or four times, overlapping, or at different angles.

Then make another tracing of it and draw into and away from this following lines as you feel.

Remove it when you think it is nearly right. Look at it critically and draw in an odd related line where you want to emphasize an area.

Define your outer limit.

Shade in on another sheet of tracing paper the shapes you wish to apply. Try different tones. Leave out what you don't want.

Try a monogram in a circle using two or more letters. Make the letters full enough to occupy most of the circle.

Drawing/tracing towards design

As a development from the ideas using shapes plus lines you can now start by drawing simply and then re-tracing. You will automatically produce something which 'holds together', something which is obviously related because it has come from the same source. As you discover these possibilities you will be able to go on with a more freehand method.

You should always work from the inside, growing outwards, extending lines so that you can take the area you like afterwards. If

Opposite: Appliquéd skirt in cotton and polyester using the letter 'r' to form a border. Designed and made by Helen Woolmer

Below: Belt showing machine zigzag and leather ties. The spaces and letters are based on the name Lesley

Bottom: Cushion cover in machine appliqué using the name Joy in a circle, by Flo Tallis

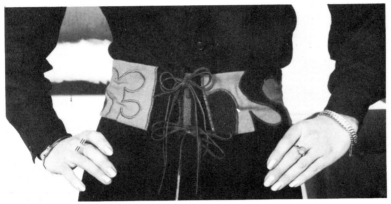

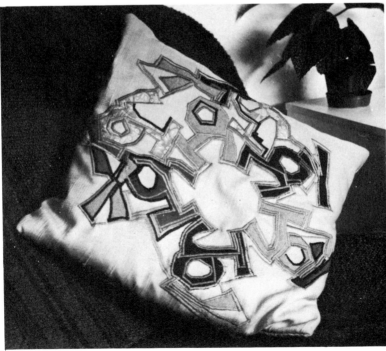

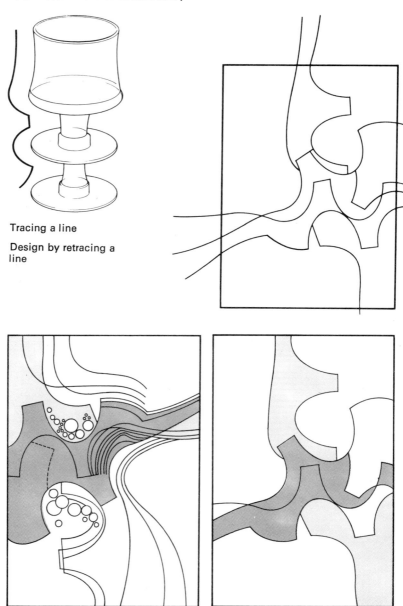

Tracing a line

Design by retracing a
line

Shading in of shapes makes an emphasis in different areas. Lines have been
added to balance the weight of the shapes

you work within a rectangle you will find it very difficult to choose where to put your lines.

Draw one line by looking at part of the outline of something in your surroundings (a bottle, say, or a chair) or put a piece of tracing paper over a photograph and draw a line that wanders from one shape to another. By this means you may have a line which is more interesting than you could have thought of yourself.

Take a larger sheet of tracing paper and draw this line in the middle Then build up on this by moving the line on your first tracing under the second sheet and keep redrawing it.

Bring the line in from further away or extend at the end (the 'growing' idea).

Overlap and so on as you feel inclined. You need not necessarily draw the whole line each time if one end, or the middle would balance best.

Keep looking each time to see if you think you have drawn enough.

Then take your 'L' corners and decide on the composition. It is now up to you to interpret it into embroidery. Which lines are stitch lines? Which lines are the outside edges of the shape?

You can add more lines in relation to what you have if you decide that most of it looks like shapes of fabric.

8. Canvas Work

Canvas work is what some people call tapestry, (needlepoint or petit-point), which must have originated from the time when canvas work hangings were stitched in order to copy the woven tapestries imported into this country.

It is embroidery worked on an open weave, stiff fabric (the canvas) which can be bought in different densities. A very close weave is hard to work on, it tends to strain the eyes and only thinner threads can be used. Anything from ten holes to about fifteen holes to an inch (2·5 cm) is easy to work on. The smaller the number of holes the fewer the threads and therefore the larger the holes, making it more difficult to cover the canvas.

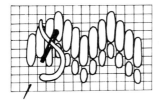

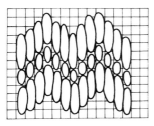

Chevron stitch

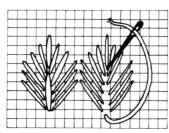

Leaf stitch

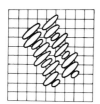

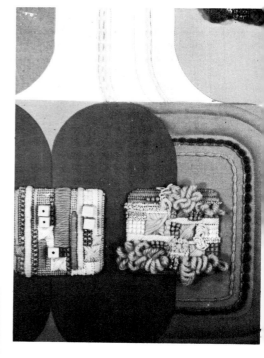

Working left to right

Working diagonally

Tent stitch

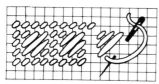

Cushion stitch

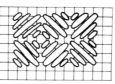

Cushion stitch variation

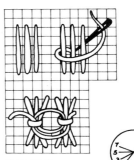

Shell stitch

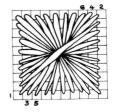

Rhodes stitch
Worked as square or rectangle

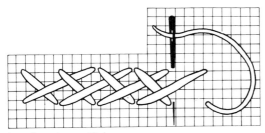

Long-legged cross stitch

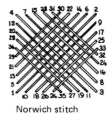

Norwich stitch

Encroaching Goblin

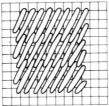

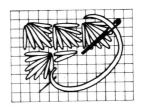

Fan stitch

Detail of panel from cut-up photo of kitchen using shapes over card and canvaswork applied with stab-stitches

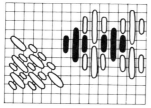

Hungarian stitch

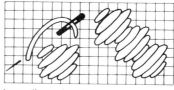

Large diagonal stitch

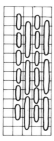

Parisian stitch

Small diagonal stitch

Melanese stitch

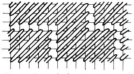

Byzantine stitch

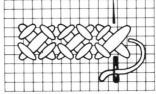

Rice stitch

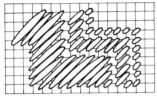

Jacquard stitch, a variation of
Byzantine stitch

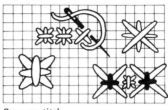

Smyrna stitch

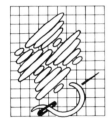

Milanese stitch

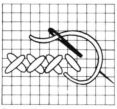

Cross stitch

Oblong cross

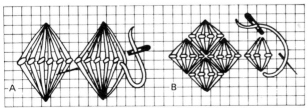

Rococo stitch

A- Tie down with a tent stitch if the threads are of uneven number

B- Tie down with back stitch if the threads are an even number

Canvas work can be used for a complete article on its own or pieces of canvas work can be applied in the same way as fabrics. As a piece of embroidery it is strong and durable, and very suitable for such articles as cushion covers, chair seats, bags, purses, belts, jewellery and boxes. If you are going to sit on your work you obviously have to be more careful about the length of stitch, the use of beads and so on. When you are to hang it on the wall and look at it you can be quite free with your textures, beads and padding.

No longer do you have to have geometric designs just because the canvas is based on squares. You can plan your work on squared paper but it does not leave you a great deal of freedom. Nowadays curves and free stitchery are quite acceptable if they fit the purpose and you understand how to cope with them. Obviously the designs are based on squares because of the weave, but the curves are made of a stepping line and when worked this is not obvious.

Whatever you are working, you should design it in the same way as your 'ordinary' embroidery. You should think of canvas work as being areas of textures, the smallest being the tent stitch.

But when we use all canvas work and no other fabrics or surfaces it can become very boring, just because there is so much texture. This is the one difficulty, that it can look too much the same all over, so you must experiment with stitches in the same way as before, varying the size and type of thread. You must think of choosing stitches as you would surfaces of fabrics, asking yourself, 'What do they look like next to each other?' and so on. All canvas stitches have directional and surface qualities like fabrics, so you need to make sure you are right before you spend the time working an area. There are stitches that have a diagonal look, vertical, horizontal, small textures, squared textures, large squared and lumpy textures, and some that are more smooth and 'all over', some come out flat and some very ridged and in relief, all these can be played one against the other. Too much colour in a piece of canvas work destroys the effect of the various textures the stitches make, so a limited colour scheme is usually better (one 'family' plus the complementary for instance).

Stitches can run into each other instead of stopping on a definite line, rather like paint on wet paper, something which is harder to do with fabric.

The only way you can get anything very smooth in canvas work is to use appliqué on the top. Either fabric over card and stab-stitched (or zigzag machined if it is a cushion cover), or leather flat or padded (as shown on page 49). Alternatively you can apply larger pieces of canvas work to a background fabric and add other embroidery.

The ideas already considered on texture and relief and use of beads can all be used in canvaswork, you just have to realize that you are working on a more open-weave fabric. Look back at Chapter 4 and try out the ribbons and other ideas.

Other types of embroidery can be incorporated (or used on top of canvaswork): needle-weaving is good for a freer effect. Such ordinary stitches as chain, twisted chain, stem stitch, Portuguese knotted-stem stitch, french and bullion knots, couching, raised-chain band and Portuguese border stitch are some that can be worked actually into the canvas rather than on top of a canvaswork stitch.

Canvaswork is best handled in a frame. The slate frame is most popular as you can work in the middle of it (page 18), sometimes the stitches pull the canvas out of line and you will need to stretch it damp as shown in the section on mounting and finishing (page 107).

A blunt needle is used and any threads as long as you double or treble them so that the stitch covers the canvas. It is only if you want to sit on it or wear it that you need to use your own discretion on threads and type of stitch, and in those cases you need to cut off the knot you started with. Start further along the line you are going to work, do a running stitch back down it and then work over that and cut the knot off when you reach it.

All the stitches should be tried in various sizes and threads so that you have a visual dictionary of surface textures for reference.

The variations work in exactly the same way as your normal embroidery stitches: widen them, enlarge them, or use two colours or shiny and dull together.

Try and remember to bring the needle through from the back of the canvas in an empty hole, and down from the right side into a filled hole. (The stitches have to cover the canvas and so each row or stitch uses the hole of the last one, otherwise a thread of canvas would be left in between.)

You must not use the needle as you would for ordinary sewing, in and out at the same time. You must pull it through first before poking the needle back the other way. Try to keep one hand below the frame and one on top, as it is quicker and creates a better tension. Never pull the thread too tight. Complete each stitch as you work it in case you need to undo a section. For instance, do not work a cross stitch by doing a row of one diagonal first and then coming back and overstitching the other; work each cross every time. If it is in two colours, you work one first and then the other over it in that case.

Whenever you have a stitch that is to finish on a curved line or a line that cuts into the pattern the stitch makes, try and work the stitch as though you had cut some off, in other words, half or two-thirds of it. Try not to fill in with tent stitch as this looks completely different and draws attention to the fact that you could not finish the stitch because of lack of space.

Remember stitches that follow the weave of the canvas need softer embroidery threads to cover the canvas: they have to fatten out to cover the canvas on either side of them, whereas diagonal stitches cover easily and are therefore good for some of the non-wool embroidery threads.

You will often need to count in order to fit stitches in. Count the holes because the needle always goes into, and comes out of, a hole. You then know you have reached the right one – remember to repeat the first and last stitch in the same hole, as you count each group – 1 2 3 4 5/1 2 3 4 5/1 2 3 4 5 and so on.

9. Finishing and Mounting

If your embroidery is worked on a frame it may go a little limp and need retightening, but it should not develop wrinkles or puckers. When you have worked it in your hand it may need stretching on a damp pad when it is finished in order to shrink out the puckers. If you feel it needs this treatment:

1. Check that your background fabric will not spoil with water.
2. Pin three or four layers of blotting paper on a board large enough for the embroidery. Wet them and drain off any excess water.

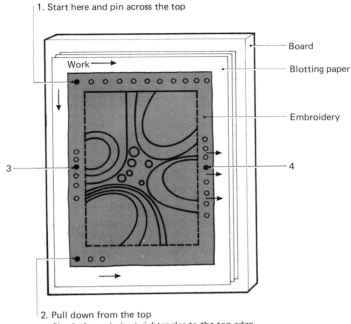

1. Start here and pin across the top

Board

Work ⟶

Blotting paper

Embroidery

3

4

2. Pull down from the top
Check the grain is at rightangles to the top edge
before putting the first pin in.

3. Lay your embroidery WS to the blotting paper. Pin it down across the top edge at intervals of 1 in./2·5 cm keeping the straight grain taut. Then pull down the bottom edge and pin that in the same way. The two sides should then be similarly treated, finishing with them straight and at right angles. This should have stretched out any unevenness in the fabric, and the dampness as it soaks in will shrink the fabric back so that the work is completely flat when dry.
4. Dry flat in an unheated place for a day or so.
5. Remove and mount.

Ideas for mounting an embroidery to hang on the wall

There are various ways of mounting and finishing when the work is stretched over card or hardboard and others suitable for work that is kept on the frame it was worked on. The following ideas are mainly for small items which are not very heavy.

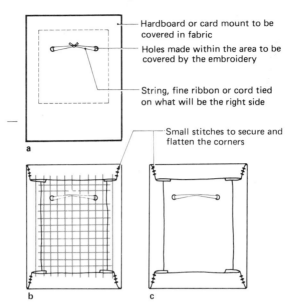

Hardboard or card mount to be covered in fabric

Holes made within the area to be covered by the embroidery

String, fine ribbon or cord tied on what will be the right side

Small stitches to secure and flatten the corners

Wrong side of mount when covered in fabric
b. String up with fine string or strong wool at least every inch
c. Glued

A hanging cord should be put through the back board before covering with backing fabric.

Using two layers

The two layers can be: card on top, hardboard underneath; cakeboard on top, card underneath; or cakeboard on top, hardboard underneath. The underneath one being larger to give a surround to the small embroidery.

The embroidery is fixed to the back of the top card with an adhesive, or strung to hardboard, the underneath card is then covered with mounting fabric.

The top can be glued to the bottom, or if it is too heavy for an adhesive it must be stitched to the mounting fabric *before* fixing over the mounting board. Some extra adhesive at the back of the embroidery will help.

Cakeboards

If you use a cakeboard as a base with no second card, the means of hanging can be either a flat loop of tape glued at either end to the back, or one that goes through the cakeboard. Because this loop goes right through the cakeboard it must be flattened and stuck to the RS of the board where it will be covered by the embroidery and the knot needed to tie the loop together left at the back (WS).

Small panel mounted on cakeboard and then on hardboard, worked by the author

Cutting mount

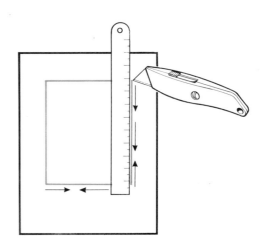

A birthday card for a lady
of 101 with a card
mount and couched
thread round the edge.
Designed and worked by
the author

Card mounts

The mount has to be cut with great care using a Stanley knife or perhaps scissors if you require a circle.

For a square cut proceed as follows:
1. On the top side mark the rectangle with extended lines in a sharp, soft pencil which will not dent the card. This is rubbed out at the end.
2. Put the point of the knife into each corner and work your way towards the centre of each side. Keep the ruler (or metal edge) on the outside, so that if the knife slips it will be inwards, in which case you will not spoil the actual mount.
3. Run the knife along gently three or four times; do not press hard until you have a groove to guide the knife.

For a circular cut you may be able to go gently round with a Stanley knife if the circle is large, by turning the card or working 3–4 in./7·5–10 cm) at a time. Otherwise use scissors and then sandpaper the edge afterwards.
4. Then fix your work to the back of the mount with an adhesive (or Sellotape), slightly stretching to keep it smooth.
5. A thread couched round the edge of the card when the embroidery is in place makes a neat finish.

Work in a card mount can be framed in an ordinary picture frame, the plainer the better.

The mount can be covered in fabric.

Fabric mount

When covering a card mount with fabric:
1. Work on a soft clean board that will take pins.
2. Put your fabric RS down and lay the card mount, with the hole cut, over that.
3. Pin with ordinary dress pins at 1 in./2·5 cm intervals about 1 in./2·5 cm away from the hole, all round. (Drawing pins spoil the fabric.)
4. Without pulling the fabric up, carefully cut out the centre to $\frac{3}{4}$ in./19 mm from the edge of the card.

Cut into the corners (not quite to the card – $\frac{1}{16}$ in./1·5 mm short), fold this turning back and stick to the card.

The pins you put in originally should help to hold the fabric in place so that you do not pull any section more than another.

a

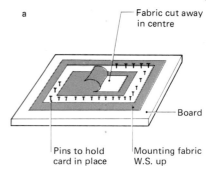

Fabric cut away
in centre

Board

Pins to hold
card in place

Mounting fabric
W.S. up

b

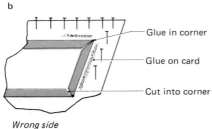

Glue in corner

Glue on card

Cut into corner

Wrong side

c

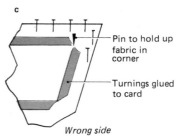

Pin to hold up
fabric in
corner

Turnings glued
to card

Wrong side

d Cross section of fabric mount

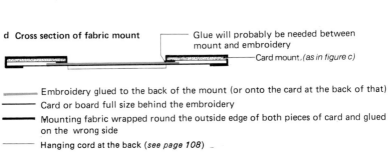

Glue will probably be needed between
mount and embroidery

Card mount. *(as in figure c)*

Embroidery glued to the back of the mount (or onto the card at the back of that)

Card or board full size behind the embroidery

Mounting fabric wrapped round the outside edge of both pieces of card and glued
on the wrong side

Hanging cord at the back (*see page 108*)

e Padded mount

Wadding layed on the card

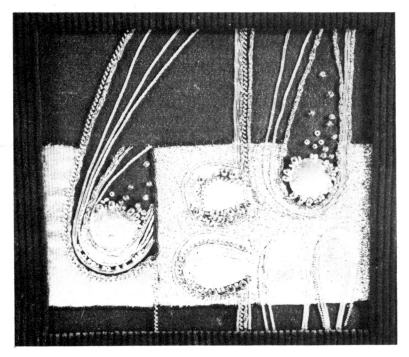

Fabric mount for box top, by the author

5. In the corners you will need to put a small amount of adhesive, on a needle, down the side of the card. Stroke the fabric up against it and put a pin in the extreme corner to keep it in place as the adhesive dries, otherwise all the frayed edges stick out and show.

6. When dry, unpin and turn over. When positioned over the embroidery the outer edge should be turned to the back of the card, frame, or whatever the embroidery was on, and glued or stapled to the back.

If the fabric is of a very loose weave and will fray easily a small piece of iron-on interlining would help where the corners come.

For a circle you will need to snip the turning every $\frac{1}{2}$ in./12 mm so that you have a smooth edge as the fabric is eased over the card.

For a padded mount, work as just suggested but lay kapok or terylene wadding between the card and fabric before stretching it over the outer edge of the embroidery when you position the mount.

For work left on the embroidery frame (home-made type)

The hanging cord can be screwed to the frame at the back afterwards.

No edging at all

When you do not want to put any edging at all round the outside the background fabric must be stretched very neatly at first.

The fold must go down the corner and not at an angle and the fabric stapled or pinned to the back out of sight.

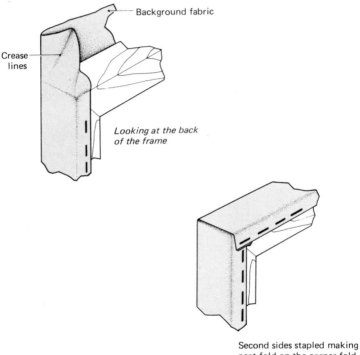

Background fabric

Crease lines

Looking at the back of the frame

Second sides stapled making neat fold on the corner fold

Wood edging

This can be wide and thin so that when viewed from the front will not be too heavy.

Use wood $\frac{1}{4}$ by $1-1\frac{1}{2}$ in./6 by 2·5–3·8 mm width. Mitre the corners and panel-pin each piece to the outside of the frame. Remember the thickness of the fabric takes up a little space. Bring the edging slightly forward from the face of the embroidery – this forms some protection when it is handled.

The wood can be left natural or painted white, gold or any colour you wish.

Fabric mount

This has been described above. If it is laid over an embroidery on a frame leave enough material to go round the side of the frame and underneath, folding the corners as in the diagram.

Fabric edging

For this use staples, (or possibly upholstery tacks).
1. Cut a strip of fabric on the straight grain – the length round the frame plus two turnings, and three times the width of the frame.

If you need more joins in the fabric put two where they are less obvious on the sides. Try to avoid joins at the corners because they will become too bulky.

You can change colour as the fabric does on the background. Simply put a seam where the change takes place.

Slide this, RS towards the embroidery, down over the frame from the top leaving the bulk of it sticking up, staple in a few places to hold it there.

Cut card strips the width of the frame and enough to go round the whole thing. Continuous lengths are not necessary.

Place the card strip on the outside. Start level with a corner and with the top surface of the embroidery. Staple in position every inch towards this top edge. Cut the card at each corner. Do not bend it round. Butt up the pieces to join as you go round and staple across the butted edges.

Ease the fabric over the card, starting with the four corners bit by bit as you work round the frame. When it is finally pulled over staple to the back of the frame folding and flattening the corners.
2. You can add a fabric-covered board to the back of this (hardboard) and probably in the same fabric as the edging. This would give weight and colour round your embroidery.

The hardboard would be screwed to the frame from the back. You may need to clamp the two together while doing this.

Steps in working a fabric
edging round an embroidery
on a homemade frame

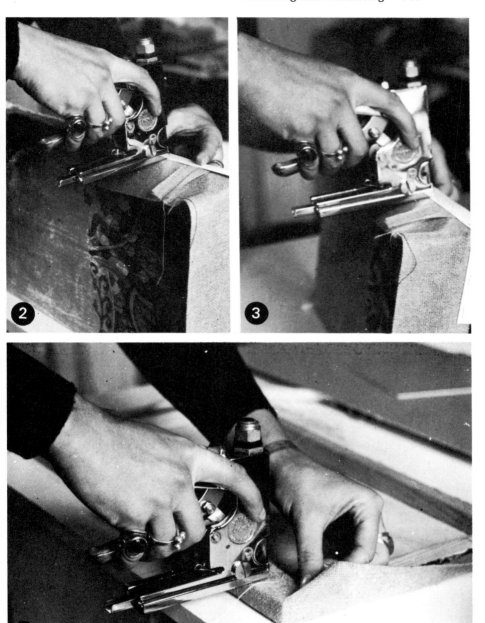

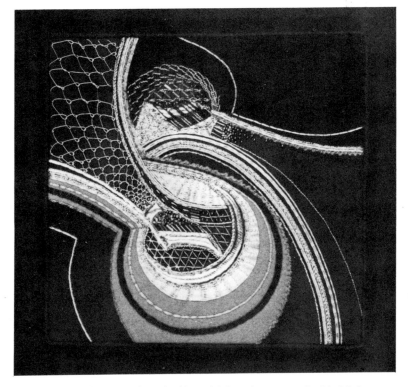

Panel based on letters and worked in gold threads, mounted with fabric edging and using the same fabric all round on hardboard as a mount. Designed and worked by Mary Caroll

Points to remember

* The mount or frame must not detract from the embroidery. It is meant to complement it.

* If the embroidery is fine, the mounting should be of an appropriate weight.

* If the embroidery is thick and heavy, woolly or shaggy, natural wood will complement it.

* If the embroidery is shiny, beaded or small, white card, fine fabric or wood painted white is suitable.

* If the embroidery has plenty of plain fabric round it, or large areas that already allow the embroidered area to stand out, it does not need any more plain fabric otherwise the area of embroidery would be diminished and overpowered.

* Likewise, if plain shapes are bold and important, anything added round the outside will upset the balance.

* The colour of the mount is also critical. If you decide to use a colour which is already in the embroidery remember from your colour work that your eye links up all the same colours. If a shape goes to the outside edge, then it merges into a mount of the same colour and does not stop at the edge. Here you might use a fabric edging that changes colour with the shapes on the edge, seamed together before stapling.

I have deliberately kept to the simple forms of embroidery in this book and if you have tried most of the ideas and actually worked several pieces then you will begin to feel you need more techniques with which to express yourself. You can still use the same design methods but the translation process will be different. The following book list will give you greater scope to develop. They are all practical books and mostly meant for those who already have experience in the basic design and techniques of embroidery.

DYER, ANNE, and DUTHOIT, VALERIE, *Canvaswork from the Start*, Bell, 1972.

MCNEIL, MOYRA, *Pulled Thread*, Mills & Boon, 1971

RHODES, MARY, *Needlepoint – the art of Canvas Embroidery*, Octopus Books, 1974

The following are all published by Batsford:

BUTLER, ANNE and DAVID GREEN, *Pattern and Embroidery*, 1970

GILTSOFF, NATALIE, *Fashion Bead Embroidery*, 1971

GREY, JENNIFER, *Machine Embroidery Technique and Design*, 1973

JOHN, EDITH, *Needleweaving*, 1970

MORRIS, MAIR, *Creative Thread Design*, 1974

NICHOLSON, JOAN, *Simple Canvaswork*, 1973

RUSSELL, PAT, *Lettering for Embroidery*, 1971

SHORT, EIRIAN, *Introducing Macramé*, 1970

SHORT, EIRIAN, *Introducing Quilting*, 1974

THOM, MARGARET, *Smocking in Embroidery*, 1972

TIMMINS, ALICE, *Introducing Patchwork*, 1972

These embroideries are all
representative: they depict
the subject while preserving
the qualities of embroidery.

Suppliers

Readers will find that their local colleges of further education or even centres of adult education will probably have classes in embroidery where the personal advice will encourage those who are a little more timid on their own. Your local library or information centre will inform you. City and Guilds and G C E examinations are likely to be offered at such colleges as well.

The following is a list of suppliers. You will need to write for catalogues, samples and information. John Lewis & Co and Liberty & Co will not have such information as they are large stores but they will, however, send samples if you know what you want.

McCullock and Wallis Limited,
25/26 Dering Street,
London W1R 0BH

John Lewis and Company Limited,
Oxford Street,
London W1X 1EX

The Needlewoman shop,
146/148 Regent Street,
London W1R 6BA

Liberty and Company Limited,
Regent Street,
London W1R 6BA

Mace and Nairn,
89 Crane Street,
Salisbury,
Wiltshire

Christine Riley,
53 Barclay Street,
Stonehaven,
Kincardineshire AB3 2AR

Limericks,
Hamlet Court Road,
Westcliff-on-Sea,
Essex

The Felt and Hessian Shop,
34 Greville Street,
London EC1

Honewill Limited,
Leather Merchants,
22a Fouberts Place,
London W1

B. and G. Leathercloth Limited
71 Fairfax Road.
London NW6 4EE

Fred Aldous Limited,
The Handicrafts Centre,
37 Lever Street,
Manchester M60 1UX

Ells and Farrier Limited,
5 Princes Street,
London W1R 8PH

Sesame Venture,
Greenham Hall,
Wellington,
Somerset

Light Leather Limited,
16 Soho Square,
London W1

Rural Industries Bureau,
Wimbledon Common,
London SW15

The Campden Needlecraft Centre,
High Street,
Chipping Campden,
Gloucestershire

Louis Grosse Limited,
36 Manchester Street,
London W1

E. J. Arnold (School Suppliers),
Butterley Street,
Leeds L210 1AX

Art Needlework Industries Limited,
7 St Michael's Mansions,
Ship Street,
Oxford

Craftsmans Mark Limited,
Broadlands,
Shortheath,
Farnham,
Surrey

Dryad Limited,
Northgates,
Leicester

Hugh Griffiths,
Brookdale, Beckington,
Bath,
Somerset

Index